The New Grammar in Action 2

Barbara H. Foley

with Elizabeth R. Neblett

Union County College
Cranford, New Jersey

HEINLE & HEINLE

THOMSON LEARNING

Australia • Canada • Mexico • Singapore • Spain • United Kingdom • United States

ACKNOWLEDGMENTS We wish to thank the faculty and students at the Institute for Intensive English, Union County College, New Jersey, for their support and encouragement during this project. Many faculty members previewed the units in their classrooms, offering suggestions for changes and additions. Students shared stories and compositions, and smiled and posed for numerous photographs. Thanks, also, to the staff at Heinle & Heinle, who remained encouraging and calm throughout the development and production of this revision.

The publication of *The New Grammar in Action 2* was directed by the members of the Heinle & Heinle Secondary and Adult ESL Publishing Team:

Managing Developmental Editor:	Amy Lawler
Production Services Coordinator:	Maryellen E. Killeen
Market Development Directors:	Jonathan Boggs and Thomas Dare

Also participating in the publication of the program were:

Vice President and Publisher, ESL:	Stanley Galek
Associate Developmental Editor:	Joyce La Tulippe
Director of Global ELT Training:	Evelyn Nelson
Manufacturing Coordinator:	Mary Beth Hennebury
Project Manager:	Hockett Editorial Service
Photo/Video Specialist:	Jonathan Stark
Interior Designer/Compositor:	Greta D. Sibley & Associates
Cover Designer:	Gina Petti/Rotunda Design House
Illustrator:	James Edwards

Manufactured in the United States of America.

ISBN: 08384-67237   10 9 8

Heinle & Heinle is a division of International Thomson Publishing, Inc.

Library of Congress Cataloging-in-Publication Data
Foley, Barbara H.
   The new grammar in action : an illustrated workbook / Barbara H.
  Foley with Elizabeth R. Neblett.
     p. cm.
  ISBN 0-8384-6723-7
   1. English language--Textbooks for foreign speakers. 2. English
language--Grammar--Problems, exercises, etc. I. Neblett, Elizabeth
R.
  PE1128.F568 1997
  428.2'4--dc21
                 97-19886
                 CIP

Photo Credits All photos by Jonathan Stark except where noted. Photos by Elizabeth R. Neblett: pages 2, 6, 1 of 3 on 7, 11, 81, 93, 110, 143, 152, 160. Photo by Stock/Boston: page 34. Photo by The Stock Market: page 44.

Contents

To the Teacher

The New Grammar in Action, a three-level grammar series for secondary and adult ESL/EFL students, offers a dynamic, communicative approach to language learning. The series presents English language structure and practice through inviting contexts such as jobs, the "average" American, marriage, working parents, and consumer buying. Bold, lively illustrations, authentic student photographs, and information-rich charts and graphs illustrate each context for practice and use of each structural focus. The series offers a wealth of variety for students and teachers to engage in both whole class and small-group activities. Listening components to each unit guide students to identify structures in context and in use, progressing from controlled presentation to more open-ended, interactive language use. Throughout the text, students are encouraged to share their ideas and experiences, to think more critically about subject matter, comparing and contrasting ideas as they gain greater control and confidence in the target language.

GRAMMAR IN ACTION

Grammar in Action sections open each unit, setting the context and grammar focus. Listening activities, accompanied by illustrations, introduce a new topic and related vocabulary. Before listening to the tape, students may be asked to practice new words and forms, describe a picture or make predictions about what they are about to hear. Students may ask to hear the listening as many times as they wish. Listening sections are structured to allow students the opportunity to follow pictures in sequence, identify words and phrases, fill in information, and comprehend natural language forms in use.

Activities in the **Grammar in Action** section are varied for whole class and pair oriented work, appealing to diverse learning styles while directing students to answer questions, complete sentences, provide information about themselves, form sentences from cues, give directions and describe illustrations. In this way, **Grammar in Action** units set the tone for high student interest and interaction during classroom time.

WORKING TOGETHER

Working Together sections give students the opportunity to work with a partner or a small group on more open-ended, communicative exercises presented within the context of the unit. Grammar is put into immediate use in the form of interviews, surveys, role plays, chart and graph skills as well as problem-solving activities. Students are encouraged towards fluency with the exchange of ideas.

Information gap exercises, identified as **Student to Student** sections, are included throughout most of the **Working Together** units. These sections allow for both controlled and open-ended practice between students. Students work in pairs, each looking at a different page. Students share and exchange ideas through challenging exercises that ask them to find information, to fill out charts and graphs, match questions and answers, and think about a topic in new ways.

PRACTICING ON YOUR OWN

Practicing on Your Own sections allow students the time to internalize the structures presented within each unit through written practice and expression. This section is useful for individual homework and review. Students gain more confidence writing and thinking in the target language as they complete cloze exercises, sentence completions, and stories with question formations. As these units continue, students progress to more exercises that ask them to contrast structures and forms of language.

SHARING OUR STORIES

Many units include **Sharing Our Stories** sections with authentic essays and narratives by and about ESL students and teachers and their experiences. These personal narratives are points of departure to stimulate student story-telling and writing. After reading these stories, students are encouraged to write about their own lives and experiences. Additionally, there are other opportunities presented throughout the text, marked by a writing icon, for students to expand on a topic or idea through their own personal written expression.

HAVING FUN WITH THE LANGUAGE

The **Having Fun with the Language** section outlines expansion activities for both in and outside of class time. Suggestions for surveys, games, interviews and research and library work give students the chance to play with language in new contexts. These units are especially helpful for students who may be wrestling with a troublesome skill or structure, as students and teachers alike can select activities of high interest and appeal.

GRAMMAR SUMMARY

These sections offer additional structural focus throughout each unit by providing an overview of the grammar for the lesson. Explanations are brief and clear, appropriate for high-beginning and low-intermediate students. Appendices at the back of the book offer additional support and reference material.

Teachers will view *The New Grammar in Action* as both a solid basis for classroom instruction and a text which allows for creative expansion of grammar structures in form and use. Over time, teachers will personalize their use of the series, expanding the units with current magazine articles, charts from newspapers, workshop ideas, and more.

Jobs

Present Tense of *Be*

 A. LISTEN: TWO JOBS *Listen to each person talk about work. Check the words that apply to the job.*

Susan is a _parking meter reader._

The work is:

☑ boring   ❑ interesting   ☑ stressful

☑ easy   ❑ difficult   ❑ creative

❑ heavy   ❑ light   ☑ tiring

The pay is:

❑ low   ❑ good

The hours are:

❑ good   ❑ bad   ❑ long

The benefits are:

❑ good   ❑ bad

Her work is:

❑ near her home   ❑ far from her home

Rosa is a _____

The work is:

❏ boring ❏ interesting ❏ stressful

❏ easy ❏ difficult ❏ creative

❏ heavy ❏ light ❏ tiring

The pay is:

❏ low ❏ good

The hours are:

❏ good ❏ bad ❏ long

The benefits are:

❏ good ❏ bad

Her work is:

❏ near her home ❏ far from her home

B. JOB INFORMATION *Use the information in Exercise A to make sentences about each person's job.*

EXAMPLE

Ana's job is boring.   The work is easy.

C. COMPLETE *Complete these sentences with **is, isn't, are,** or **aren't.***

Be	
I	am
He She It	is
We You They	are

1. Susan __is_____ a meter reader.

2. People _____ happy to see her.

3. Sometimes, the weather _____ a problem.

4. The work _____ difficult, but it _____ interesting, either.

5. Her hours _____ great.

6. Rosa _____ a small business owner.

7. The largest part of her business _____ special occasions.

8. The work _____ boring.

9. Her customers _____ happy with their flower arrangements.

10. The hours _____ long, so it _____ easy to take a vacation.

◼ D. YES/NO QUESTIONS *Sit with a partner. Ask and answer these questions about Susan and Rosa.*

Susan:

1. Are people happy to see Susan?
2. Is the weather always nice?
3. Is her job interesting?
4. Are her hours good?
5. Are her benefits good?

Rosa:

1. Is Rosa's work difficult?
2. Is her work creative?
3. Are the customers happy with her work?
4. Is it difficult to be a small business owner?
5. Are her benefits good?

◼ E. WORK EXPERIENCE *Complete these sentences about your work experience. Read them to a partner.*

1. I am a/an _____ .

2. I work at _____ in _____ .

3. My work is   **boring   interesting.**

4. My hours are   **good   bad   long.**

5. I work from ___:___ to ___:___ .

6. My benefits are   **good   bad.**

7. My work is   **near my home   far from my home.**

8. In my country, I was a/an _____ .

■ PREPOSITIONS OF PLACE

	in		on		at
room	in the living room in Room 211 in the office	street	on Main Street on Broad Street	buildings	at the store at the bank at the post office
city state country	in Boston in Ohio in the United States in Canada	floor around the house	on the first floor on the fifth floor on the porch on the deck	buildings (exceptions— do not use *the*)	at work at school at church at home
around the house	in the yard in the basement in the garage in the attic			an address	at 12 North Avenue at 426 Center Street

EXAMPLES

He works **on** Broad Street.

He works **at** 338 Broad Street.

The address is 338 Broad Street.

■ F. PREPOSITIONS *Refer to the chart above and complete each sentence with **in, on,** or **at.***

1. He works ___in___ Cincinnati.

2. His office is _____ the seventh floor, room 71.

3. George is _____ work now.

4. Sofia works _____ 54 Park Place.

5. The office building is _____ York Street.

6. The headquarters of the company is _____ San Francisco. There are branch offices _____ Taiwan and Japan.

7. The company has representatives _____ Canada, Mexico, and throughout Europe.

8. Peter isn't _____ his office now. He's _____ the bank.

9. Some employees of our company work _____ home.

10. After work, I sit _____ the deck and relax.

G. LISTEN: NUMBERS *Listen and complete each sentence with the number you hear.*

1. He works on the ___ninth___ floor.

2. He's in room _____ .

3. Her address is _____ Maple Avenue.

4. She's on the _____ floor, in apartment _____ .

5. They work at _____ North Union Avenue.

6. She works in the Medical Building, at _____ Spring Street.

7. Her office is on the _____ floor, in room _____ .

8. I was on the _____ floor last year, but now I'm on the _____ floor in room

   _____ .

9. The address is _____ Treemont Drive.

10. She is at _____ Weston Avenue.

first
second
third
fourth
fifth
sixth
seventh
eighth
ninth
tenth

■ H. ANSWER *Answer these questions. Use a preposition in your answer.*

1. Where are you now? What floor are you on?
2. Where do you live? What's your address?
3. Where's your school? What street is it on?
4. Where's your doctor? Where's your dentist?
5. Do you have any relatives in the United States? Where do they live?
6. Where do you work? Where is your company or business?

■ A. CHOOSING A JOB *Talk about the jobs in the photographs using the adjectives below.*

boring	interesting	difficult	easy
tiring	stressful	dangerous	high
low	long	bad	good

1. This job is _____.

2. The pay is _____.

3. The hours are _____.

4. The benefits are _____.

5. I would/wouldn't like this job because _____.

B. WHAT'S IMPORTANT IN A JOB? *You are looking for a job or deciding on a career. What is most important to you? Rank these characteristics in order from 1 to 7.*

_____ The job is close to my home.

_____ The salary is good.

_____ The benefits are good.

_____ The work is interesting.

_____ My co-workers are friendly.

_____ There is a possibility for a promotion.

_____ The hours are good for me.

Sit in a group and discuss your top three choices. Are there any characteristics you all think are important? What jobs have these characteristics?

C. STUDENT TO STUDENT

Who is a _____ ?
What is _____ ?
What's his/her address?
What floor is his/her office on?
What's his/her office number?

Student A: Use the chart below.

Student B: Turn to page 181.

You both have a chart of four workers, but some of the information is missing. Ask and answer questions to complete your charts.

	Job	Address	Floor	Office
Mrs. Baker		431 Pine Street		275
Ms. Brown	Lawyer			1092
	Engineer		third	346
Ms. Wilson	Accountant		seventh	732
Mr. Perez		948 Lake Street		

D. INTERVIEW *Interview a student in your group who works and complete the chart.*

Where do you work?

What do you do?

How do you like your job?

How is your boss?

How are your benefits?

Practicing on Your Own

A. COMPLETE *Complete with the correct pronoun and preposition.*

Pronouns
he—his
she—her
they—their
Prepositions
in   on   at

EXAMPLE

There are many doctors ___at___ the Medical One Center.

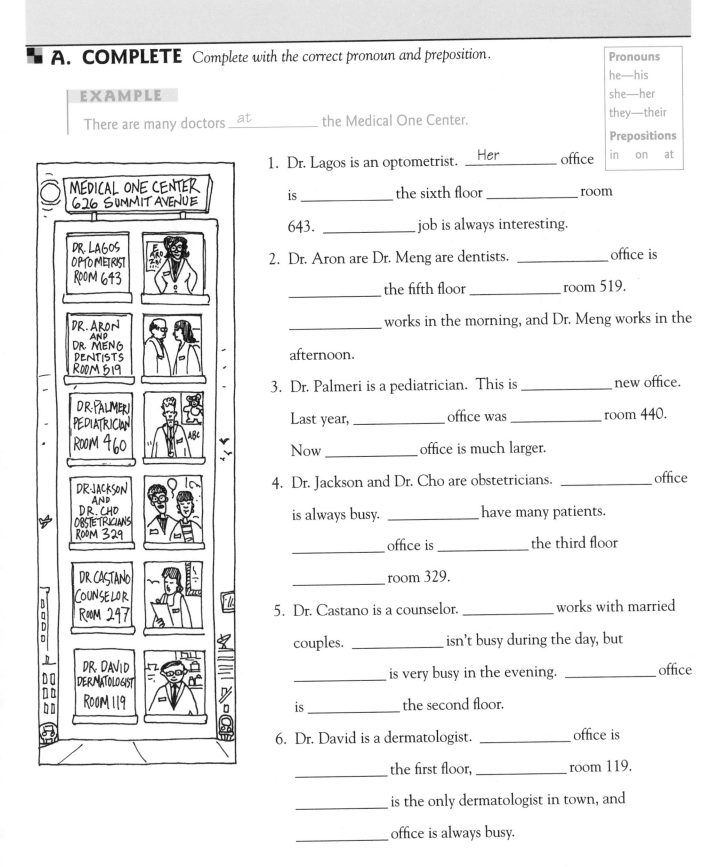

1. Dr. Lagos is an optometrist. __Her__ office
   is _____ the sixth floor _____ room
   643. _____ job is always interesting.

2. Dr. Aron are Dr. Meng are dentists. _____ office is
   _____ the fifth floor _____ room 519.
   _____ works in the morning, and Dr. Meng works in the
   afternoon.

3. Dr. Palmeri is a pediatrician. This is _____ new office.
   Last year, _____ office was _____ room 440.
   Now _____ office is much larger.

4. Dr. Jackson and Dr. Cho are obstetricians. _____ office
   is always busy. _____ have many patients.
   _____ office is _____ the third floor
   _____ room 329.

5. Dr. Castano is a counselor. _____ works with married
   couples. _____ isn't busy during the day, but
   _____ is very busy in the evening. _____ office
   is _____ the second floor.

6. Dr. David is a dermatologist. _____ office is
   _____ the first floor, _____ room 119.
   _____ is the only dermatologist in town, and
   _____ office is always busy.

1. Is this building at 62 Summit Avenue?   _No it isn't._____

2. Is Dr. Lagos a dermatologist?   _____

3. Is her office on the second floor?   _____

4. Is her job interesting?   _____

5. Are Dr. Aron and Dr. Meng dentists?   _____

6. Is their office in room 519?   _____

7. Are they both in the office all day?   _____

8. Is Dr. Palmeri in a new office?   _____

9. Is his new office in room 460?   _____

10. Is his new office larger?   _____

Now write five more questions and answers about this medical building.

■ **C. PREPOSITIONS** *Complete these sentences with* **in, on** *or* **at.**

1. Sandra works __at___ Marvin Plastics. The building is _____ 317 Grove
   Street. Her office is _____ the second floor _____ room 244.

2. Darrell works _____ an accounting firm _____ Park Avenue.

3. Nancy lives _____ 127 Jefferson Street. She works _____ the same street.
   Her office is _____ 456 Jefferson Street.

4. Larry works _____ Flagg Plaza, _____ the tenth floor of the building. Flagg
   Plaza is _____ Second Street _____ Springfield.

5. Bernice's office was _____ the fifth floor. She now works _____ the third
   floor _____ room 355.

6. Charles lives _____ Pennsylvania, but he works over the border _____ New
   Jersey.

7. Diana isn't _____ work today. She's _____ home.

8. I'm sorry. Mr. Richards isn't _____ the office today. He's _____ a meeting
   _____ Boston.

Read this story about Armin, a salesperson and distributor of telephone calling cards.

Telephone calling cards are a new business and they have become very popular. First, thousands of people do not have telephones in their homes. Also, people don't like receiving a large telephone bill from their phone company. And finally, if people use a public phone, they don't need to carry a lot of change with them.

I am a telephone card salesperson. I sell telephone calling cards to distributors, stores, and businesses. I travel all day, stopping at about 15 to 20 locations. Some of these places are convenience stores or delis. Many restaurants now carry calling cards. People eat out for dinner and relax, and then they want to go home and call their families.

My car is my office. I carry a laptop computer with me and keep all my accounts on my computer. I represent about ten calling card companies. Each of my customers buys between 30 and 100 cards a week on consignment. The next week, when I return, they pay me for the cards they sold. The store gets a commission and I get a commission. I work long hours, six or seven days a week. I like being my own boss. You can be a successful salesperson, too. You need to be friendly, organized, and ambitious.

Armin Torres

Write about your own job or the job of one of your friends or relatives. What do you do? Where do you work? What city is your company in? What are your hours? What do you like about your job? What don't you like?

Having Fun with the Language

◼ A. FAMOUS PEOPLE

*These are the names of well-known people. How many do you know? Tell what each person **is** or **was**.*

> **EXAMPLE**
>
> Picasso was a painter.
> Pavarotti is a singer.

Pablo Picasso	Oprah Winfrey	Gabriel García Márquez
Luciano Pavarotti	Martin Luther King, Jr.	Steven Spielberg
Bill Clinton	Marie Curie	Colin Powell
Sandra Day O'Connor	I.M. Pei	Amy Tan
Lady Diana Spencer	Nelson Mandela	Frederic Chopin
John Paul II	Margaret Thatcher	Thomas Edison
Martina Navaratilova	Jackie Chan	William Shakespeare

Your group should think of the names of ten more famous people. Present them to another group. Do they know who each person is?

Grammar Summary—*Be* Statements

◼ I. Statements

I	am	
He		
She	is	
It		at work.
We		
You	are	
They		

Negatives

I	am not	
He		
She	is not	
It	isn't	in the office.
We		
You	are not	
They	aren't	

2. Contractions

I am → I'm
he is → he's
she is → she's
it is → it's
you are → you're
they are → they're
we are → we're
is not → isn't
are not → aren't

Examples

I'm in the living room.
He's in my class.
She's in the basement.
It's on the first floor.
You're at school.
They're on the main floor.
We're at the bank.
She **isn't** on Main Street.
They **aren't** at 12 North Avenue.

3. *Yes/no questions*

Am I at school?
Are you in the office?
Is he in the yard?
Is she at work?
Is it on Park Avenue?
Are we on Broad Street?
Are you at home?
Are they in Canada?

Short answers

Yes, you are.	No, you aren't.	No, you're not.
Yes, I am.	No, I'm not.	
Yes, he is.	No, he isn't.	No, he's not.
Yes, she is.	No, she isn't.	No, she's not.
Yes, it is.	No, it isn't.	No, it's not.
Yes, you are.	No, you aren't.	No, you're not.
Yes, we are.	No, we aren't.	No, we're not.
Yes, they are.	No, they aren't.	No, they're not.

2 The Average American

Present Tense

A. SOME STATISTICS
Read each sentence about an average American. Try to guess the correct answer. Circle it.

> The average American (represents a typical person)—singular
> Most Americans (represents 75% or more of Americans)—plural

1. The average American sleeps   **7   8   9**   hours a night.
2. The average American watches   **2   3   4**   hours of TV a day.
3. Most Americans go to the dentist   **once   twice   three times**   a year.
4. Most Americans drive to work. The average commute is   **25   35   45**   minutes.
5. The average American eats   **1   2   3**   hamburger(s) a week.
6. The average American drinks   **1   2   3**   cup(s) of coffee a day.
7. The average American earns   **$16,000 $22,000 $30,000**   a year.
8. The average American eats at a fast-food restaurant   **1   2   3**   time(s) a month.
9. The average American drinks   **1   2   3**   can(s) of soda a day.
10. Most American families rent   **2   4   6**   movies a month.
11. Most Americans have   **1   2   3 or more**   credit card(s).
12. The average American moves   **3   7   11**   times in a lifetime.

Check your answers on page 25. If your guess was wrong, cross it out and circle the correct answer. Did any of the information surprise you?

B. LISTEN: CHARLIE
Listen to Charlie describe himself and his lifestyle. You will need to take a few notes. Compare Charlie to the average American male.

> **Present Tense**
> Charlie is
> Charlie weighs

Charlie	The Average American Male
32—single	gets married at 26
	5'9" tall (men)
	162 pounds
	likes his or her job
	works 8 hours a day
	earns $28,500
	lives in a house
	drives to work
	has a pet, usually a cat or a dog

■ C. CHARTS AND GRAPHS *Look at the charts and graphs and circle the correct answer.*

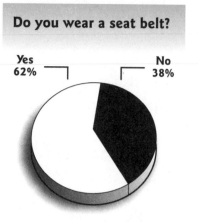

Do you wear a seat belt?

Yes 62%   No 38%

1. The average person **wears**   **doesn't wear**   a seat belt.

2. Most people **wear**   **don't wear**   a seat belt.

3. I **wear**   **don't wear**   a seat belt.

4. My teacher **wears**   **doesn't wear**   a seat belt.

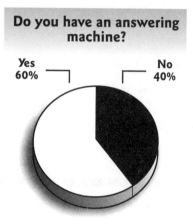

Do you have an answering machine?

Yes 60%   No 40%

5. The average home **has**   **doesn't have**   an answering machine.

6. Most people **have**   **don't have**   an answering machine.

7. I **have**   **don't have**   an answering machine.

8. My teacher **has**   **doesn't have**   an answering machine.

Do you have a fax machine?

Yes 8%   No 92%

9. The average home **has**   **doesn't have**   a fax machine.

10. I **have**   **don't have**   a fax machine.

11. My teacher **has**   **doesn't have**   a fax machine.

Do you like to cook?

Yes

Men 56%   Women 78%

12. The average man **likes** **doesn't like** to cook.

13. Most women **like** **don't like** to cook.

14. I **like** **don't like** to cook.

15. My teacher **likes** **doesn't like** to cook.

■ **D. THE AVERAGES** *Read these sentences about the average American. Then listen to your teacher talk about his or her life. Is your teacher "average"? Circle* **Yes** *or* **No** *for each item. Now circle* **Yes** *or* **No** *about yourself. Make sentences about your teacher. Make sentences about yourself. Compare your answers.*

> **Present Tense**
> The average American lives in a house.
> My teacher lives in a house.
> My teacher doesn't live in a house.
> I live in a house
> I don't live in a house.
> I live in an apartment.

The Average American	My Teacher		Me	
1. The average American lives in a house.	Yes	No	Yes	No
2. The average American works 8 hours a day.	Yes	No	Yes	No
3. The average American reads the newspaper every day.	Yes	No	Yes	No
4. The average American has a pet.	Yes	No	Yes	No
5. The average American eats pasta once a week.	Yes	No	Yes	No
6. The average American uses an ATM* machine.	Yes	No	Yes	No
7. The average American spends $92 a year on lottery tickets.	Yes	No	Yes	No
8. Most Americans eat cereal for breakfast.	Yes	No	Yes	No
9. Most Americans have checking accounts.	Yes	No	Yes	No
10. Most Americans read one or more magazines a month.	Yes	No	Yes	No
11. Most Americans do not speak a second language.	Yes	No	Yes	No
12. Most Americans have a VCR.	Yes	No	Yes	No

*ATM—automatic teller machine

Working Together

A. INTERVIEW *Sit with a partner. Answer these questions; then circle the correct information for you and your partner.*

1. Do you own a computer?

    a. I **own   don't own**   a computer.

    b. My partner **owns   doesn't own**   a computer.

2. Do you wear a seat belt?

    a. I **wear   don't wear**   a seat belt.

    b. My partner **wears   doesn't wear**   a seat belt.

3. Do you have a credit card?

    a. I **have   don't have**   a credit card.

    b. My partner **has   doesn't have**   a credit card.

4. Do you have a pet?

    a. I **have   don't have**   a pet.

    b. My partner **has   doesn't have**   a pet.

5. Do you work full time?

    a. I **work   don't work**   full time.

    b. My partner **works   doesn't work**   full time.

Answer these questions; then complete the correct information for you and your partner.

6. Do you have a fax machine?

    a. I _____ a fax machine.

    b. My partner _____ a fax machine.

Present: have			
I		He	has
You	have	She	doesn't have
We	don't have	It	
They			

7. Do you read the newspaper every day?

    a. I _____ the newspaper every day.

    b. My partner _____ the newspaper every day.

18

8. How often do you go to the dentist?

   a. I _____ to the dentist _____ a year.

   b. My partner _____ to the dentist _____ a year.

Present: read			
I		He	reads
You	read	She	doesn't read
We	don't read	It	
They			

9. How many hours a night do you sleep?

   a. I _____ _____ hours a night.

   b. My partner _____ _____ hours a night.

10. How many cans of soda do you drink a day?

   a. I _____ _____ can(s) of soda a day.

   b. My partner _____ _____ can(s) of soda a day.

B. STUDENT TO STUDENT

Student A: *Ask these questions about the average American* **man.** *Listen to Student B's answers and write the correct number on the line.*
Student B: *Look at page 181.*

1. How tall is the average _____ ? _____' _____"

2. How much does the average _____ weigh? _____ pounds

3. What is the life expectancy of an average _____ ? _____ years

4. What shoe size does the average _____ take? _____

5. At what age does the average _____ get married? _____ years old

6. How much does the average _____ earn? $_____

7. How many books does the average _____ read a year? _____

When you finish, **Student B** *will ask questions about the average American* **woman** *and complete the information above.* **Student A** *will look at page 181 and say the answers.*

■ C. GRAPHS *Sit with a partner and write three or more sentences about each graph.*

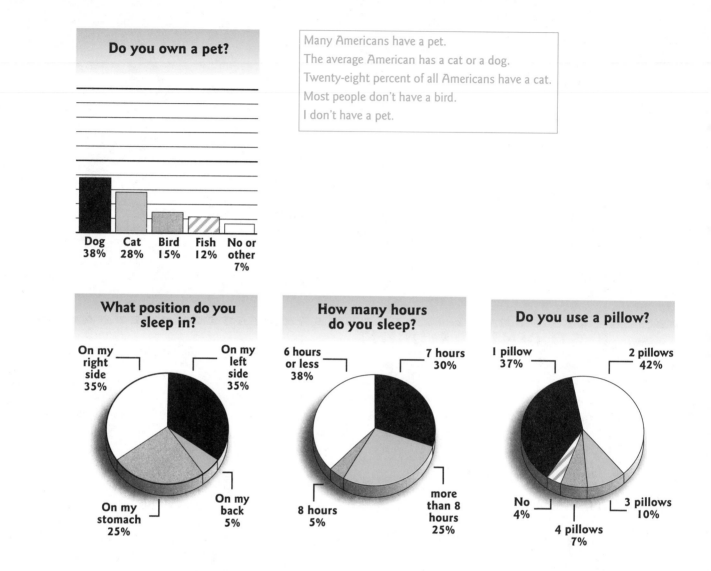

Do you own a pet?

Many Americans have a pet.
The average American has a cat or a dog.
Twenty-eight percent of all Americans have a cat.
Most people don't have a bird.
I don't have a pet.

Dog 38% Cat 28% Bird 15% Fish 12% No or other 7%

What position do you sleep in?

On my right side 35%
On my left side 35%
On my stomach 25%
On my back 5%

How many hours do you sleep?

6 hours or less 38%
7 hours 30%
8 hours 5%
more than 8 hours 25%

Do you use a pillow?

1 pillow 37%
2 pillows 42%
No 4%
4 pillows 7%
3 pillows 10%

Practicing on Your Own

■ A. PRESENT TENSE *Circle the correct form of the verb.*

1. The average American **believe** (**believes**) in God.

2. The average American **don't go**   **doesn't go**   to church every Sunday.

3. The average American **vote**   **votes**   in presidential elections.

4. Most Americans **keep**   **keeps**   their money in a bank.

5. The average American **have**   **has**   a savings account.

6. Most Americans **live** **lives** in the city or the suburbs.

7. The average American **don't live** **doesn't live** on a farm.

8. Most Americans **work** **works** eight hours a day.

9. Most Americans **like** **likes** their jobs.

10. The average worker **receive** **receives** health insurance.

11. Most Americans **drive** **drives** to work.

12. The average American **wear** **wears** a seat belt.

■ B. CHARTS AND GRAPHS *Use the information in the charts to complete these sentences.*

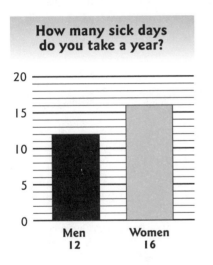

How many sick days do you take a year?

Men 12
Women 16

1. The average man _____ 12 sick days a year.

2. The average woman _____ 16 sick days a year.

3. Women _____ more sick days than men.

4. I _____ _____ sick days a year.

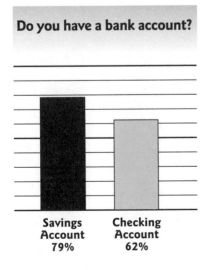

Do you have a bank account?

Savings Account 79%
Checking Account 62%

5. The average person _____ a checking account.

6. Most people _____ a savings account.

7. Seventy-nine percent of all people _____ a savings account.

8. Many people _____ both a checking account and a savings account.

9. I _____ a savings account.

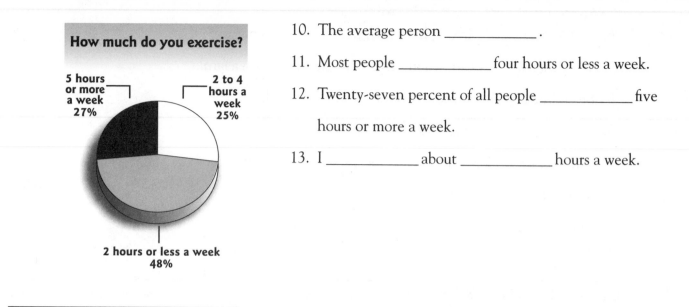

How much do you exercise?

5 hours or more a week 27%

2 to 4 hours a week 25%

2 hours or less a week 48%

10. The average person _____ .

11. Most people _____ four hours or less a week.

12. Twenty-seven percent of all people _____ five hours or more a week.

13. I _____ about _____ hours a week.

■ **C. AN AVERAGE AMERICAN** *Read this story about a typical American teenager and write the present tense form of the verb in parentheses.*

Max __is_____ (be) a typical high school student. He _____ (go) to school five days a week from September to June. Most American high school students _____ (attend) school ten months a year. They _____ (have) time off for a few national holidays, Christmas, and of course, the summer vacation. Max _____ (want) to go to college after he _____ (graduate), so he _____ (take) English, biology, American history, geometry, French, and physical education. Like many other high school students, Max _____ (participate) in extracurricular activities. He _____ (play) the clarinet in the school concert band and _____ (be) on the baseball team. Many high school students _____ (join) teams or clubs during high school. The average high school student _____ (belong) to at least one club or team. Max _____ (have) a part-time job, too. He _____ (work) at the music store downtown on Friday and Saturday evenings, but he only _____ (work) until 8:00. He still _____ (have) time for his studies and for a social life. Most high school students _____ (study) about an hour and a half a night, so Max _____ (have) to save time for his studies. He _____ (have) to have good grades to go to college.

22

Sharing Our Stories

Interview an American friend, neighbor, or student in your school who works.

Before the interview, develop a list of ten questions in your class. For example: Do you work? Please tell me about your job. What do you like to do in your free time? Tell me about your family. Now write a short paragraph about the person you interviewed.

Having Fun with the Language

A. THE HANDBAG *The typical woman carries a bag or purse, often filled to overflowing. Sit with a partner and try to guess the eight most common items that a typical woman carries in her bag or purse. Check your answers on page 25.*

_____   _____   _____

_____   _____   _____

_____   _____

B. THE AVERAGE PERSON FROM MY COUNTRY *Sit in groups of four or five students who are from **the same country.** Write seven sentences about the average person from your country. Be specific in your sentences. For example, write about **the average Mexican man** or **the average Japanese teenager.***

Read two or three of your sentences to the class. After each sentence, your classmates will tell about their own countries—for example:

EXAMPLE

The teenagers in my country study a lot.

The teenagers in my country study a lot, too.

People in my country drink tea.

People in my country don't drink tea; they drink coffee.

Grammar Summary

1. Simple present tense *The simple present tense talks about routine actions. These actions happen every day, every weekend, every week, etc.*

2. Statements

I We You They	drive	
	don't drive	to work.
He She It	drives doesn't drive	

EXAMPLES

I sleep seven hours a night.

We don't have a dog.

He likes his job.

He doesn't drive to school.

3. Singular and plural expressions

Singular	Plural
The average woman works.	Many women work.
The average man works.	Most men work.
The average person works.	Some people work.
	Seventy percent of all women work.

◾ 4. Spelling of third person, singular

Verb ending		Spelling
1. Most verbs		Add **s.**
walk	→	walks
eat		eats
come		comes
2. Verbs that end with **ch, sh, ss, x, zz**		Add **es.**
fix	→	fixes
brush		brushes
watch		watches
3. Verbs that end with a consonant and **y**		Change the **y** to **i**, add **es.**
study	→	studies
dry		dries
4. Exceptions		Memorize!
do	→	does
go		goes
have		has

Answers for Unit 2

B. Some Statistics (page 15)

1. The average American sleeps **7** hours a night.
2. The average American watches **4** hours of TV a day.
3. Most Americans go to the dentist **twice** a year.
4. Most Americans drive to work. The average commute is **25** minutes.
5. The average American eats **3** hamburgers a week.
6. The average American drinks **2** cups of coffee a day.
7. The average American earns **$22,000** a year.
8. The average American eats at a fast-food restaurant **3** times a month.
9. The average American drinks **1** can of soda a day.
10. Most American families rent **4** movies a month.
11. Most Americans have **3 or more** credit cards.
12. The average American moves **11** times in a lifetime.

Having Fun with the Language (page 23)

A. The average handbag or purse contains keys, wallet, checkbook, calendar, glasses, lipstick, pen, and gum or candy.

Present Tense Questions

A. LISTEN: GETTING TO SCHOOL *Listen and write the name of each person and the number of minutes it takes to get to school.*

Ali and George   Ann   Patty

David   Susan and Paul   Lee

Present Tense
He walk**s**.
They walk.

How long does it take?
It takes **him** one hour.
It takes **her** one hour.
It takes **them** one hour.

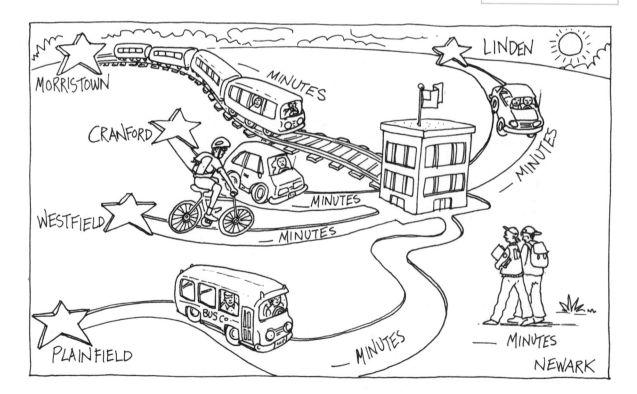

B. YES/NO QUESTIONS *Answer these questions about the picture.*

1. Does Ann live in Cranford?

2. Does she walk to school?

3. Does it take her 15 minutes?

4. Do Ali and George live in Plainfield?

5. Do they walk to school?

6. Does it take them one hour?

7. Does Lee live in Westfield?

8. Does he drive to school?

9. Does it take him 25 minutes?

10. Do Susan and Paul live in Newark?

11. Do they drive to school?

12. Does it take them 10 minutes?

C. LISTEN: QUESTIONS *Listen and write the question you hear. Circle the correct answer.*

Present Questions	
Where do they live?	Where does she live?
How do they get to school?	How does she get to school?

1. Where does Patty live _____?

   a. In Morristown.   b. By train.   c. In Plainfield.

2. _____?

   a. She walks.   b. By train.   c. 30 minutes.

3. _____?

   a. In Morristown.   b. By train.   c. 30 minutes.

4. _____?

   a. They walk.   b. In Newark.   c. 5 minutes.

5. _____?

   a. Yes, they do.   b. They're early.   c. They walk.

6. _____?

   a. 5 minutes.   b. They live nearby.   c. They walk.

Now listen to two personal questions. Write the question and your answer.

7. _____ ?

   _____

8. _____ ?

   _____

Write five more questions in the present tense about other students in the picture. Ask your partner the new questions.

■ ADVERBS OF FREQUENCY

100%	always
	usually
	often
	sometimes
	seldom
	rarely
	hardly ever
0%	never

> Place adverbs of frequency *before the verb*.
> He **always comes** to school late.
> She **seldom feels** tired.
> Place adverbs of frequency *after be*.
> He **is never** late.
> She **is often** tired.
> Note: We can also place **sometimes** at the beginning of a sentence.

■ D. ADVERB PLACEMENT *Say each sentence again. Place the adverb in the correct position in the sentence.*

       always

1. David ⌃ takes the bus to school. (always)

2. He gets up on time. (rarely)

3. He is tired in the morning. (usually)

4. He misses the bus. (often)

5. He is late for school. (often)

6. Ali and George walk to school together. (always)

7. Ali's sister drives them. (sometimes)

8. They are early for class. (usually)

9. They stop and get coffee and donuts. (sometimes)

10. Lee rides his bicycle to school. (hardly ever)

11. He is late. (seldom)

◼ E. ANSWER *Answer these questions about transportation. Use an adverb of frequency.*

How often do you take the train?
Do you ever take the train?
I take the train about once a month.   *or*
I sometimes take the train.

1. Do you ever walk to school?

2. Do you ever take the bus to school?

3. Are you ever late for class?

4. Do you ever give someone a ride?

5. Are you ever tired in class?

6. How often do you take a bus?

7. How often do you take a taxi?

8. How often do you wear your seat belt?

Working Together

◼ A. DISCUSSION QUESTIONS *Sit in a group and discuss these questions.*

1. Do you own a car? What kind of car do you have? How old is your car? What kind of expenses do you have with your car? Where do you drive? Do you take drives on the weekends to visit friends or family? Where do they live? How long does it take you?

2. Do you walk a lot? Where do you walk? Do you walk to school? To work? To town? If so, how long does it take you? Do you live near a nice park to walk in? About how many miles do you walk a week?

◼ B. INTERVIEW *Interview a student who has a car. Ask these questions and check the responses.*

	Always	Often	Sometimes	Seldom	Never
1. Do you ever have car problems?	❏	❏	❏	❏	❏
2. Do you ever fix your own car?	❏	❏	❏	❏	❏
3. Do you ever change your car's oil?	❏	❏	❏	❏	❏
4. Do you ever lose your keys?	❏	❏	❏	❏	❏
5. How often do you drive long distances?	❏	❏	❏	❏	❏
6. How often do you drive to other states?	❏	❏	❏	❏	❏
7. How often do you ask for directions?	❏	❏	❏	❏	❏
8. How often do you use a map?	❏	❏	❏	❏	❏
9. How often do you get lost?	❏	❏	❏	❏	❏

Write five sentences about the driver and show them to him or her. Is the information correct?

C. STUDENT TO STUDENT *Ask and answer questions about how these people commute to work in Chicago. Complete the chart.*

Student A: *Look at the chart on page 31.*

Student B: *Look at the chart on page 182.*

> **EXAMPLE**
>
> Where does Amy live?
>
> How does she get to work?
>
> How long does it take her?

	Town	Transportation	Time
Amy	Cicero	the El	30 minutes
Brian			
Lisa and Silvia	Bedford Park	bus	50 minutes
Matthew and Ed			

Practicing on Your Own

■ **A. PRESENT TENSE** *Complete each sentence with the correct form of the verb. Then write the questions.*

Twins

Kate _____lives_____ (live) in Los Angeles, and her twin sister, Kim,

_____ (live) in San Francisco. They _____ (visit) each

other twice a year. Each summer, Kate _____ (drive) up to San

Francisco and _____ (stay) with her sister for a week. And each year,

on February 10th, Kim _____ (fly) down to Los Angeles, and they

_____ (celebrate) their birthday together.

1. ___Where does Kate live_____? In Los Angeles.

2. _____? Twice a year.

3. _____? In the summer.

4. _____? She flies.

5. _____? It's their birthday.

31

Bus Ride

Tien _____ (live) about five miles from school. He

_____ (own—negative) a car, so he _____ (need) to

take public transportation. Unfortunately, the bus _____ (run—

negative) near his house, so he _____ (have) to walk one mile to the

nearest bus stop. The bus only _____ (stop) once an hour. When he

_____ (miss) the bus, he _____ (be) late for his

classes.

1. _____ ? About five miles.

2. _____ ? No, he doesn't.

3. _____ ? No, it doesn't.

4. _____ ? Once an hour.

5. _____ ? When he misses the bus.

■ B. ADVERBS *Answer these questions. Include an adverb of frequency in each answer.*

1. How often do you walk to school?

   _____

2. How often do you take the bus or subway to school?

   _____

3. How often do you get a ride to school?

   _____

4. How often do you drive to school?

   _____

5. Do you listen to the radio when you drive?

_____

6. Is the traffic heavy in the morning?

_____

7. Is it easy to get a parking space at school?

_____

8. Is your car messy?

_____

9. How often do you wash your car?

_____

10. Do you wear your seat belt?

_____

■ C. HOW DO AMERICANS GET TO WORK? *Answer these questions about the chart.*

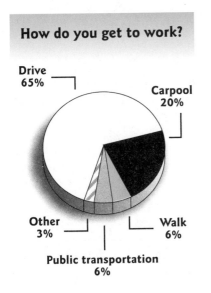

How do you get to work?

Drive 65%
Carpool 20%
Other 3%
Walk 6%
Public transportation 6%

1. How do most Americans get to work?
2. What does *carpool* mean? What percentage of people carpool?
3. Do many people walk to work?
4. In what parts of the country do you think public transportation is popular?
5. Give two examples of other types of transportation.

Read Mario's story about walking to school in the morning.

    Every school day, after breakfast, Tom and I walk to school. We usually leave at 7:30. We live on the same street, so we like to walk to school together. We almost always walk to school. If it rains, one of our parents gives us a ride. Once a week, we stop at the donut shop on the way to school. We would like to go more often, but our mothers don't like us to eat too much junk food. It's a mile to school, and it takes us about 20 or 30 minutes. We don't walk very fast; we take our time, talking to friends along the way.

    When Tom and I get to school, it's about 8:00. We go to our lockers to put our coats away. Then we hang out in the hallway with our friends. When the bell rings, we go to our homerooms. Homeroom begins at 8:20.

Mario DeLeon

Write a paragraph about coming to school. What time do you leave your house? How do you get to school? How is the traffic? If you take public transportation, is it on time? Is it crowded? How long does it take you to get to school? What time do you arrive at school? (Remember, the more details you include, the more interesting your story will be.)

Having Fun with the Language

■ **A. VEHICLES** *Sit in a group of three or four students. Your group has five minutes. How many different kinds of vehicles can you name? Can your group name more than twenty vehicles? Which group can list the most?*

> **EXAMPLE**
>
> bicycle, motorcycle, bus, helicopter...

B. GETTING FROM HERE TO THERE

Which city are you in now? Write the names of five other cities in your state. About how far is each city from here? How long does it take to drive to that city? How else can you get there?

City	Distance	Time to drive	Transportation

Grammar Summary

1. Present Tense: *Yes/no questions* Short answers

	I / you / we / they		
Do	I you we they	work?	
Does	he she it		

Yes, you do.   No, you don't.
Yes, I do.   No, I don't.
Yes, we do.   No, we don't.
Yes, they do.   No, they don't.
Yes, he does.   No, he doesn't.
Yes, she does.   No, she doesn't.
Yes, it does.   No, it doesn't.

2. *Wh* questions   Answers

When **do** you **leave?**   At 8:00.

How **does** he **get** to school?   He takes the bus.

Where **does** she **live?**   In Springfield.

How long **does** it **take?**   Twenty minutes.

When **do** we **arrive?**   At 8:30.

When **do** they **get** there?   At 9:00.

4 The States

Singular and Plural

A. LISTEN: GEORGIA *Listen to a description of Georgia. As you listen, write the number of each feature, location, or product in the circles on the map below.*

1. Appalachian Mountains
2. Blue Ridge Mountains
3. plateau
4. Atlanta
5. coastal plain
6. peanuts
7. peaches
8. Okefenokee Swamp

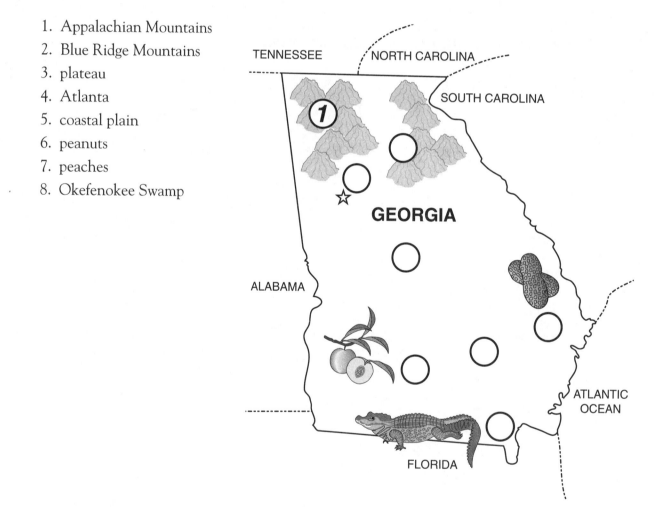

B. LISTEN: SINGULAR OR PLURAL *Circle the letter of the noun you hear.*

1. a. mountain   (b.) mountains   7. a. peach   b. peaches
2. a. city   b. cities   8. a. state   b. states
3. a. peanut   b. peanuts   9. a. industry   b. industries
4. a. area   b. areas   10. a. bird   b. birds
5. a. summer   b. summers   11. a. class   b. classes
6. a. home   b. homes   12. a. person   b. people

C. SPELLING *Write the plural of these words. Refer to the spelling chart on page 49.*

farm   _farms_ _____   lake   _____

beach   _beaches_ _____   peach   _____

bridge   _____   valley   _____

tornado   _____   canyon   _____

river   _____   volcano   _____

village   _____   desert   _____

tourist   _____   city   _____

country   _____   coast   _____

border   _____   earthquake _____

factory   _____   industry   _____

swamp   _____   cave   _____

D. GENERALIZATIONS *Generalizations state facts. Circle the correct verb in each general statement below . Look carefully at the subject to decide if the verb is singular or plural.*

1. A plateau (is) are   a raised area of flat land.

2. Climate **describes** describe   the typical weather of an area.

3. In the Northeast, seasons **changes** change   four times a year.

4. Bridges **crosses** cross   over rivers or roads and **connects** connect   two bodies of land.

5. A tunnel **cuts**   **cut**   through a mountain or under the ground.

6. Millions of tourists   **travels**   **travel**   in the summer.

7. Tropical rain forests   **grows**   **grow**   near the equator where it is very hot and wet.

8. An earthquake   **shakes**   **shake**   the earth, at times causing great damage.

9. Streams   **is**   **are**   flowing bodies of water, smaller than rivers.

10. Valleys   **is**   **are**   areas of low land that   **lies**   **lie**   between mountains.

◼ E. GENERALIZATIONS *Generalizations can be singular or plural.*

EXAMPLE

A tourist spends a lot of money.   Tourists spend a lot of money.

A desert is a hot, dry area.   Deserts are hot, dry areas.

Change these generalizations from singular to plural. The underlined object should also be made plural.

1. A desert receives very little rain.
2. An ocean is home to thousands of animals and plants.
3. A dairy farm produces milk.
4. A map shows a flat <u>picture</u> of a round world.
5. A volcano is often inactive for a hundred years or more.
6. A plain is flat or gently rolling land.
7. A river usually begins in the mountains.

Change these generalizations from plural to singular. The underlined objects should also be made singular.

| Use **a** or **an** with a singular noun. |

1. Farmers grow fruits and vegetables.
2. Rivers provide water for irrigation.
3. Dams produce electric energy.
4. Forests contain many kinds of trees.
5. Caves are underground <u>holes</u>, usually in the side of a mountain.
6. Major cities often develop around <u>bays</u> or <u>harbors</u>.
7. Bridges are <u>structures</u> that cross <u>rivers</u> or <u>roads</u>.

Make generalizations with these words. Make both a singular and the plural sentence with each.

tornado   beach   jungle

lake   swamp   hurricane

COUNT AND NON-COUNT NOUNS

<table>
<tr><td>

Count nouns are items that we can count individually (one by one). They can be singular or plural:

Examples:

    peach—peaches
     river—rivers
     farm—farms

</td><td>

Non-count nouns are only singular. They include:

1. Liquids or gases (water, oil, oxygen)
2. Items that are too small or too numerous to count (sand, corn, snow)
3. General categories (furniture, scenery, music, traffic)
4. Abstract ideas (information, beauty, life, work)

</td></tr>
</table>

F. CLASSIFY *Write these nouns under* **Count** *or* **Non-count.**

mining	traffic	weather	corn
product	crime	resort	map
season	population	beach	culture
rain	island	farming	machinery
climate	geography	wood	equipment

Count	Non-count
product	mining
season	rain

Add three more words to each column.

39

G. LISTEN: MONTANA
Look at this feature map of Montana and listen to the description. Complete the sentences by circling **is** *or* **are,** *then use one of the quantifiers from the boxes below.*

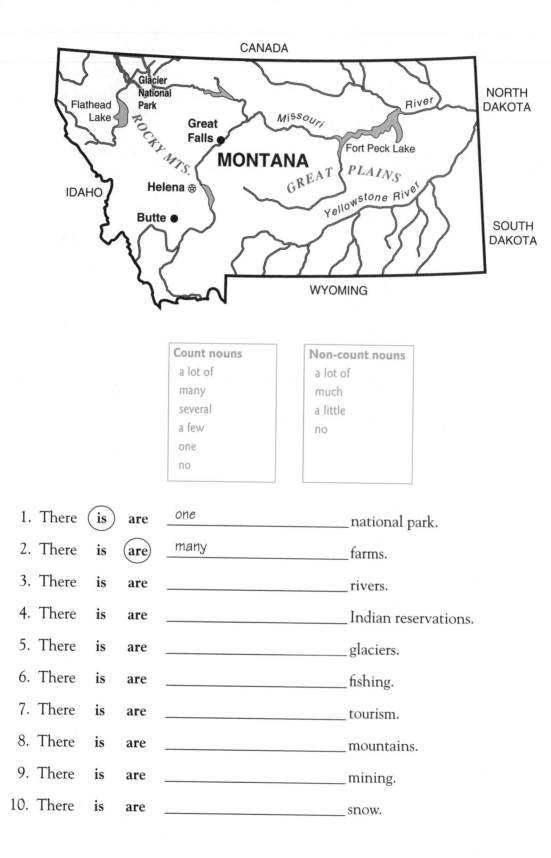

Count nouns	Non-count nouns
a lot of	a lot of
many	much
several	a little
a few	no
one	
no	

1. There ⓘs   are   _____one_____ national park.

2. There   is   ⓐre   _____many_____ farms.

3. There   is   are   _____ rivers.

4. There   is   are   _____ Indian reservations.

5. There   is   are   _____ glaciers.

6. There   is   are   _____ fishing.

7. There   is   are   _____ tourism.

8. There   is   are   _____ mountains.

9. There   is   are   _____ mining.

10. There   is   are   _____ snow.

■ H. MY STATE   *Ask and answer questions about your state with the words and phrases below.*

Count Nouns

Are there *any* lakes in (state)?
Are there *a lot of* lakes in (state)?
Are there *many* lakes in (state)?
  Yes, there are *a lot of* lakes.
  Yes, there are *a few* lakes.
  No, there aren't.

Non-count Nouns

Is there *any* pollution in (state)?
Is there *a lot of* pollution in (state)?
Is there *much* pollution in (state)?
  Yes, there is *a lot of* pollution.
  Yes, there is *a little* pollution.
  No, there isn't.

lakes	**pollution**	**cities**	**forests**
mountains	**farming**	**tourism**	**deserts**
	national parks	**traffic**	

Complete these questions about your state with **much** *or* **many;** *then circle* **is** *or* **are.** *Answer the questions.*

Count Nouns

How many lakes are there in (state)?
  There are a lot.
  There are many.
  There are a few.
  There aren't any.

Non-count Nouns

How much pollution is there in (state)?
  There is a lot.
  There is a little.
  There isn't any.

1. How ___much___ rainfall (is) are there in _____?

2. How _____ rivers is are there in _____?

3. How _____ snowfall is are there in _____?

4. How _____ traffic is are there in _____?

5. How _____ Indian reservations is are there in _____?

6. How _____ volcanoes is are there in _____?

7. How _____ tourism is are there in _____?

8. How _____ dams is are there in _____?

9. How _____ swamps is are there in _____?

10. How _____ industry is are there in _____?

Working Together

A. STATE MAP
Work together as a group. Draw a rough outline of your state on a large piece of paper. Include the following:

1. Draw your state capital.
2. Name and locate five major cities.
3. Locate and label the largest airport in your state.
4. Write your present location on the map.
5. Write in the bordering states and oceans.
6. Draw in two or three major rivers in blue. Name them.
7. Add the major lakes in your state.
8. Show mountains with ∧∧∧∧∧ and forests with 🌲🌲🌲🌲🌲 .
9. Locate any national parks that are located in your state.
10. Mark and name any major geographical features, such as canyons, swamps, and deserts.
11. Show major farm areas and list products that your state produces.
12. Indicate two major highways or routes that travel through most of your state.

B. DISCUSSION
Answer these questions about your state.

Why did you choose to live in your state?

What features do you like about your state? What features don't you like?

Do you like the weather?

What interesting places have you visited?

C. MORE OR LESS
Does your state need more of each of these items? Or does it need fewer (or less)?

EXAMPLE	
Count	**Non-count**
We need more parks.	We need more sunshine.
We need fewer highways.	We need less rain.

rain	sunshine	traffic	prisons
parks	factories	colleges	crime
snow	roads	tourism	pollution
jobs	noise	resorts	cars

D. STUDENT TO STUDENT
*Student A will look at the chart below, and **Student B** will look at the chart on pp. 182–183. You each have different facts about the largest state, Alaska. Ask and answer questions with **How much** or **How many** and complete the information in your chart.*

Student A: How many islands are there in Alaska?
Student B: There are 1,800 islands.

Alaska	
islands	1,800
volcanoes	80
glaciers	
lakes	3 million
rivers	
national parks	8
snowfall	
rain	13 inches a year in the interior
people	
Eskimos	45,000
oil	
heavy industry	a little
traffic	
fishing	a lot

A. THE MISSISSIPPI RIVER *Circle the correct verb.*

The Mississippi River ((is) are) the longest river in the United States. It (flows flow) 2,300 miles from Minnesota to New Orleans on the Gulf of Mexico. The name Mississippi (comes come) from an Indian word that means "Big water."

The Mississippi (provides provide) a transportation route for farm and industrial products going up and down the river. Goods (travels travel) from the center of the nation to the Gulf of Mexico. Tugboats (pushes push) barges, which are large, flat boats, up and down the river. These barges (is are) arranged in large convoys, sometimes with one hundred or more barges joined together.

The Mississippi (serves serve) other purposes, also. It (provides provide) water for irrigation for farming. Large refining companies (needs need) thousands of gallons of water to process oil. People (fishes fish) the waters, weekend boaters

(speeds   speed   ) up and down the banks, and bird watchers (keeps   keep   )

track of the hundreds of species of birds that stop at the river on their way north or south.

The Mississippi (does   do   ) not always (flows   flow   ) peacefully along.

Flooding (occurs   occur   ) at times of heavy rain. Levees, which are walls built along

the river, (protects   protect   ) hundreds of miles of towns, homes, and farms. In

other areas, spillways (drains   drain   ) high water into floodways or reservoirs. But

the Mississippi (has   have   ) a mind of its own, and major floods still (occurs

occur   ) from time to time.

■ **B. SINGULAR AND PLURAL** *Change these statements from* **plural** *to* **singular.**

1. Hurricanes bring heavy rain and strong wind.

    A hurricane brings heavy rain and strong wind.

2. Weather maps illustrate the weather forecast.

    _____

3. Thermometers measure the temperature.

    _____

4. Meteorologists study the weather.

    _____

Change these statements from singular to plural.

5. A tornado is a strong, violent wind.

    _____

6. A reservoir stores water for an area's use.

    _____

7. A flood covers dry land with water.

    _____

8. A volcano causes great destruction when it erupts.

    _____

■ C. HOW MUCH, HOW MANY
Write ten questions and answers about New Mexico using this feature map and chart information. Start each question with **How much** *or* **How many.** *Use a quantifier in your answer.*

How much rainfall is there in New Mexico?
There is very little rainfall.

How many ranches are there in New Mexico?
There are many ranches.

	New Mexico
Rainfall	dry, 10 to 20 inches a year
Snow	heavy in the mountains, over 300 inches a year
Reservations	more than ten Indian reservations
Colleges	nine
Ranches	Cattle is an important industry.
Farming	too dry for farming
National parks	Carlsbad Caverns
Lakes	only a few
Rivers	major rivers: Rio Grande, Pecos, San Juan, Canadian, and Gila
Mining	major industries: natural gas, petroleum, gold, copper
Tourism	major industry
Mountains	Rocky Mountains

1. _____How much_____ snow _____is there_____ in New Mexico?
   _____There is a lot of snow._____

2. _____ reservations _____ in New Mexico?
   _____

3. _____ colleges _____ in New Mexico?
   _____

4. _____ farming _____ in New Mexico?
   _____

5. _____ national parks _____ in New Mexico?

_____

6. _____ lakes _____ in New Mexico?

_____

7. _____ rivers _____ in New Mexico?

_____

8. _____ mining _____ in New Mexico?

_____

9. _____ tourism _____ in New Mexico?

_____

10. _____ mountains _____ in New Mexico?

_____

Sharing Our Stories

Lydia Garcia used information in the library to help her write about her state, California. Read her description.

California: The Golden State

I live in San Diego, California. California is on the Pacific Ocean, and it's the third largest state. The population (1995) is over 31 million people. A lot of different people live in California. The population (1990) is 69% white, 25.8% Hispanic, 9.6% Asian, and 7.4 % black.

Along the coast, the weather is beautiful. The temperatures are moderate. In the interior, there are both mountains and deserts. California is also famous for its bad weather, however. Sometimes there is too much rain in the north and too little rain in the south. Earthquakes are a serious concern in my state. Most earthquakes are small, but major earthquakes can destroy buildings, roads, and bridges in a few seconds.

Agriculture is a major industry in California.

California grows more than half of the nation's fruits and vegetables. I can buy fresh fruit all year. California has many industries. Aircraft, electronic equipment, and computers are a few of them. I work at a computer company and assemble computer parts.

I especially love California because I can spend all of my free time outdoors. In my town, people fish, surf, sail, and play tennis. I like to roller blade along the boardwalk near the beach.

Lydia Garcia

 Write a description of your state. Use the information from Working Together (A.) to help you. You can also find information in the library, in an encyclopedia, CD-ROM reference materials, and an almanac. Write about the location, population, geographical features, parks, and weather. What other interesting information can you find?

Having Fun with the Language

A. FOLLOWING THE NEWS
Place a map of the United States on the wall or bulletin board. Follow the national news headlines with your class for a month or more. Where is the news happening? Use string to make a "line" from the headline (real or printed on an index card) to the state and city. Mark headline news events, natural disasters, sports championships, presidential visits, etc.

Grammar Summary

1. Count nouns

1. **Use**

   Count nouns are items that we can count individually, one by one. They can be singular or plural.

   town—towns
   city—cities
   lake—lakes

Non-count nouns

1. **Use**

   Non-count nouns cannot be counted individually. They are only singular. They include:
   1. Liquids or gases (water, oil, oxygen)
   2. Items that are too small or too numerous to count (sand, corn, snow)
   3. General categories (furniture, scenery, music, traffic)
   4. Abstract ideas (information, beauty, life, work)

1. Count nouns (continued)

2. Quantifiers

For a count noun, we can count the exact number or use one of the quantifiers below:

a lot of	There are a lot of farms.
many	There are many rivers.
a few	There are a few parks.
one	There is one lake.
no	There are no deserts.

3. *Yes/no* questions

For a singular noun, use *Is there a* and the singular noun:

> Is there a desert in your state?
> Yes, there is.
> No, there isn't.

For a plural noun, use *Are there* and the plural noun:

> Are there any deserts in your state?
> Yes, there are.
> No, there aren't.

4. *How many* questions

Use *How many* for a count noun:

> How many lakes are there in your state?
> There is only one.
> There are only a few.

Non-count nouns

2. Quantifiers

For a non-count noun, use one of the quantifiers below:

a lot of	There is a lot of traffic.
much	There is much snow.
a little	There is a little industry.
no	There is no noise.

3. *Yes/no* questions

Use the singular form to ask a question:

> Is there much traffic in your state?
> Yes, there is.
> No, there isn't.

4. *How much* questions

Use *How much* for a non-count noun:

> How much rain is there in your state?
> There is a lot of rain.
> There isn't much rain.

2. Spelling

Noun Ending		Spelling
1. Most nouns		Add **s**
farm	→	farms
area		areas
state		states
2. Nouns that end with **ch, sh, ss, x, zz**		Add **es**
beach	→	beaches
class		classes
3. Nouns that end with a consonant and **y**		Change the **y** to **i,** and add **es.**
city	→	cities
industry		industries
4. Irregulars		Memorize!
man	→	men
woman		women
person		people
child		children

5 The Airport

Present Continuous

Grammar in Action

A. LISTEN: THE AIRPORT *Listen and write each name under the correct picture.*

Charles   Kathy and Lisa   Jessica   Amanda   Megan

Ben   Mark   Brian   Chris   John

> **Present Continuous**
> The present continuous tense describes an action that is happening now.

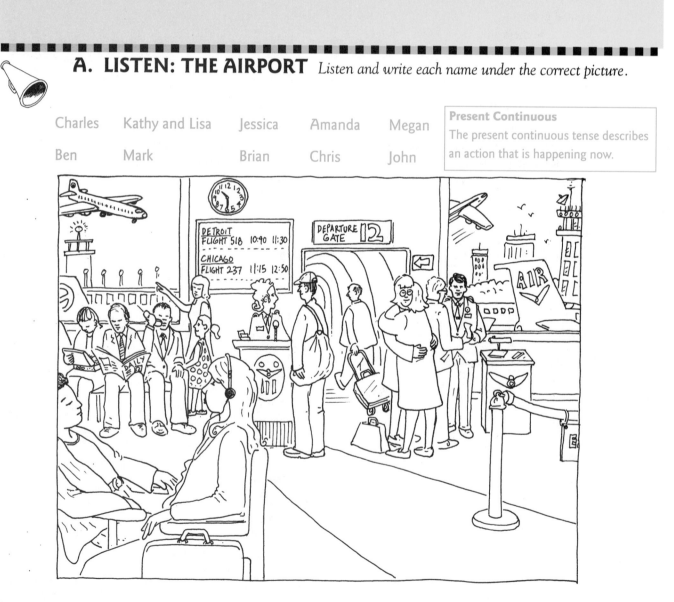

50

B. DESCRIBE THE PICTURE *Use these verbs to describe what each person is doing now.*

Charles is boarding the plane.

Kathy and Lisa are saying good-bye to each other.

wait	walk	pull	hand
say	stand	sit	talk
watch	read	listen	sleep
use	give	check	ask

Present Continuous			
I	am		
He			
She	is		waiting for a plane
It			
We			
You	are		
They			

C. CORRECT IT! *Find the mistake in each sentence, and then say the sentence correctly.*

Brian is reading <u>a book</u>.

Brian <u>isn't reading</u> a book.

He's reading <u>the newspaper</u>.

Kathy and Lisa are saying <u>hello</u>.

Kathy and Lisa <u>aren't saying</u> hello.

They're saying <u>good-bye</u>.

1. Charles is carrying his suitcase.
2. Ben is leaving the plane.
3. Kathy and Lisa are boarding the plane.
4. Mark is talking to the pilot.
5. Jessica and her daughter are watching a plane take off.
6. Brian is wearing jeans.
7. Amanda is using her fax machine.
8. Chris and Megan are talking.
9. Chris is not sleeping.
10. John is talking to his boss.

D. YES/NO QUESTIONS *Ask and answer questions about the people in the airport. Use any name(s) in the blanks.*

Is Charles sleeping?

Yes, he is

No, he isn't.

Are Kathy and Lisa talking?

Yes, they are.

No, they aren't.

1. Is _____ sleeping?

2. Is _____ giving his/her ticket to the attendant?

3. Are _____ and _____ talking?

4. Is _____ getting on the plane?

5. Are _____ and _____ watching the planes land?

E. LISTEN: QUESTIONS *Listen and write the question you hear. Then circle the correct answer.*

Present Continuous Questions
Why **is** he **sleeping?**
Where **are** they **sitting?**

1. _Where is Mark standing_____ ?

    a. On the plane. (b.) At the check-in desk.   c. By the window.

2. _____ ?

    a. Mark is.   b. To the attendant.   c. Yes, he is.

3. _____ ?

    a. A ticket.   b. The attendant.   c. A window seat.

4. _____ ?

    a. By the window.   b. The planes.   c. Yes, they are.

5. _____ ?

    a. At the airport.   b. They're pointing.   c. The planes.

Write five more questions in the present continuous about the airport. Ask a partner your questions.

■ **NON-ACTION VERBS** *Some verbs in English do not usually take the present continuous. They are non-action verbs.*

hate	appear	agree	belong
like	feel	believe	cost
love	hear	forget	have
prefer	look (to appear)	know	need
	see	(not) mind	
	smell	remember	
	seem	think	
	sound	understand	
	taste		

■ F. CONTRAST
Complete these sentences about people who are flying or who are at the airport. Use the present continuous or the present (non-action).

1. Mark ___is talking___ (talk) to the flight attendant. He ___wants___ (want) a seat near the window.

2. Jack is on the plane, and he _____ (eat) the chicken dinner. It _____ (smell) delicious, but it _____ (taste) terrible.

3. Laura _____ (sit) in the last row of the plane. The flight is bumpy, and she _____ (feel) sick.

4. Karl _____ (sit) in his seat, and _____ (hold) onto the arm rests. He _____ (hate) to fly.

5. Jeff _____ (relax) in a private airport lounge. He _____ (belong) to the Frequent Fliers Club.

6. The flight _____ (go) smoothly. The pilot _____ (think) the plane will arrive early.

7. Kim _____ (need) to use the restroom, but several people _____ (wait) in line.

8. Thomas _____ (buy) a ticket to Guatemala. It _____ (cost) $690.

9. Javier _____ (listen) to the safety instructions, but he _____ (understand—negative) anything.

Working Together

■ A. DISCUSSION
Sit in a small group and talk about the nearest major airport.

1. What is the nearest major airport? Is it an international airport?
2. How far is the airport from you? How long does it take you to get there? How do you get to the airport?
3. How large is the airport? Is it usually busy?
4. Does the airport have good parking?
5. What major airlines operate in and out of the airport?
6. How often do you go to the airport? When was the last time you were there? Were you picking up or dropping off someone?

B. CUSTOMS PROBLEMS

The Gibsons are returning from a trip abroad and are going through Customs. Sit in a group of three students and write a story about what is happening. Use your imagination, the Vocabulary Box, and the questions under the picture to help you.

Vocabulary Box

search

inspect

Customs official

Customs dog

sniff

Who is arriving? Where are they coming from? What's the Customs official doing? What's he holding? What are they saying? Why is the dog sitting by the suitcase? How do the Gibsons feel? What's going to happen to this family?

C. STUDENT TO STUDENT

Ask and answer questions about the flights and fill in the missing information.

Student A: Look at the Flight Board on page 55.

Student B: Look at the Flight Board on page 183.

When is flight 643 arriving/leaving?

What gate is it arriving at?

Which flight is going to Atlanta?

Where is Delta flight 824 going?

What gate is flight 643 arriving at?

FLIGHT BOARD

Arrivals					Departures				
Northwest	643	Chicago	3:50	34			Atlanta		54
Northwest	716	Toronto			Delta	824		4:25	62
Continental	278	Seattle			Delta	721			71
Continental	455	Denver	6:35	24	Delta	336	Miami	5:15	44

Practicing on Your Own

■ A. COMPLETE *Look at the opening picture on page 50 and complete these sentences with the present continuous form of the verb.*

wait	land	hug	board	walk
travel	hand	fly	take	pull

1. The flight to Detroit _is boarding_____ now.

2. Several people _____ for the flight to Chicago.

3. Charles _____ onto the plane.

4. He _____ his carry-on luggage onto the plane.

5. Ben _____ his ticket to the flight attendant.

6. He _____ to Denver for a business meeting.

7. Kathy and Lisa _____ each other.

8. Jessica and her daughter _____ for the plane to Chicago.

9. They _____ to Chicago to visit her parents for a week.

10. Planes _____ and _____ off every few minutes.

■ B. PRESENT CONTINUOUS
Write five affirmative and five negative sentences about Larry and Susan's flight. Use your imagination and the phrases in the box to help you.

eating

smoking

talking

flying to

coming from

sitting

reading a magazine

listening to music

wearing a seat belt

enjoying the flight

watching a movie

■ C. COMPLETE THE STORY
Complete the story with the correct form of the present continuous or present tense. Then write the questions.

It's 10:00 A.M., and the Atlanta airport is crowded and busy. Flight 534 __is boarding_____ (board) now. The plane is full. In fact, the flight is overbooked; there are 250 seats and 251 passengers. Janet West is the extra passenger. She _____ (have—negative) a seat, and she _____ (look) very upset. Her daughter _____ (come) home from the hospital this afternoon with her first child. She _____ (want) to be there when her daughter arrives home. The check-in clerk _____ (announce) that the airline _____ (look) for one passenger to take the 12:00 flight. They _____ (offer) a free ticket to anywhere in the continental United States to the volunteer. Tom Larson _____ (offer) to wait. He _____ (have) a business meeting in Miami, but not until this evening. He still has plenty of time to get to his meeting. With his free ticket, he _____ (plan) to visit his brother in Arizona.

1. <u>How many passengers are there?</u>

   There are 251.

2. _____

   Very upset.

3. _____

   This afternoon.

4. _____

   One free ticket.

5. _____

   Tom Larson is.

6. _____

   To visit his brother in Arizona.

Having Fun with the Language

■ A. WHERE ARE THEY COMING FROM? *These passengers just got off different airlines and are returning home. What is each person carrying or wearing? Guess the city or place each person is returning from.*

What would a visitor bring back from your city or state?

Grammar Summary

▪ I. Present continuous tense

In the present continuous tense, we talk about an action that is happening **now**:

> The passengers **are waiting** for the plane.

If an action is in the near future or is a definite future plan, the present continuous can have a future meaning:

> The plane **is arriving** in ten minutes.

> My husband **is meeting** me at the airport.

▪ 2. Some present continuous time expressions

now   right now   at the present time

▪ 3. Statements

I	am am not	studying.
He She It	is isn't	working.
We You They	are aren't	talking.

▪ 4. *Yes/no* questions   Short answers

Am I **waiting?**	Yes, you are.	No, you aren't.	No, you're not.
Are you **buying** a ticket?	Yes, I am.	No, I'm not.	
Is he **boarding** the plane?	Yes, he is.	No, he isn't.	No, he's not.
Is she **waiting** in line?	Yes, she is.	No, she isn't.	No, she's not.
Is it **landing?**	Yes, it is.	No, it isn't.	No, it's not.
Are we **getting** off?	Yes, you are.	No, you aren't.	No, you're not.
Are you **leaving?**	Yes, we are.	No, we aren't.	No, we're not.
Are they **reading?**	Yes, they are.	No, they aren't.	No, they're not.

▪ 5. *Wh* questions   Answers

Wh questions	Answers
When **am** I **leaving?**	At 5:40.
What **are** you **reading?**	A magazine.
What **is** he **watching?**	A movie.
When **is** it **taking** off?	In ten minutes.
Where **are** we **sitting?**	In row 24.
Where **are** you **walking?**	To the rest room.
What **are** they **doing?**	Checking tickets.

▪ 6. Spelling

Verb ending		Spelling
1. Most verbs		Add **ing.**
walk	→	walking
eat		eating
carry		carrying
2. Verbs that end with **e**		Drop the **e** and add **ing.**
write	→	writing
take		taking
3. One-syllable verbs that end with a consonant, vowel, consonant		Double the final consonant and add **ing.**
sit	→	sitting
run		running
Do not double **x, y,** or **z**		
buy	→	buying

6 Everyone Is Present

Indefinite Number

A. LISTEN: THE CLASSROOM Listen to these sentences about the classroom. Circle *True* or *False*.

1. True   False
2. True   False
3. True   False
4. True   False
5. True   False
6. True   False
7. True   False
8. True   False

9. True   False
10. True   False
11. True   False
12. True   False
13. True   False
14. True   False
15. True   False

B. ANSWER Answer these questions about your classmates. Use **everyone, someone** or **no one** in your answer.

> *Everyone, No one,* and *someone* are singular.
> Everyone **is** present.
> Someone **is** at the door.
> No one **is** wearing a hat.

EXAMPLE

Is anyone absent today?   No one is absent today.

1. Is anyone absent today?

2. Is anyone at the door?

3. Is anyone talking?

4. Is anyone standing at the blackboard?

5. Is anyone using a dictionary?

6. Is anyone reading?

7. Is anyone raising his or her hand?

8. Is anyone studying English?

9. Is anyone listening to the answers?

10. Is anyone tired?

◼ C. ALL . . . NONE *Repeat these sentences after your teacher. Ask about the meaning of any new words or phrases.*

1. All of the men are wearing hats.

2. Most of the men are wearing hats.

3. Many of the men are wearing hats.

4. Some of the men are wearing hats.

5. A few of the men are wearing hats.

6. A couple of the men are wearing hats.

7. One of the men is wearing a hat.

8. None of the men is wearing a hat.

◼ D. MY CLASSMATES *Complete these sentences about your classmates. Use an expression from the box on the right. Circle the correct verb. Write two more sentences.*

Quantifiers
All of us
Most of us
Many of us
Some of us
A few of us
A couple of us
One of us
None of us

1. _____   **is   are**   from Mexico.

2. _____   **is   are**   married.

3. _____   **is   are**   under 20 years old.

4. _____   **works   work**   part time.

5. _____   **has   have**   blond hair.

6. _____   **has   have**   brown eyes.

7. _____   **is   are**   wearing sneakers.

8. _____   **likes   like**   to play soccer.

9. _____   **wears   wear**   glasses.

10. _____ **is** **are** over six feet tall.

11. _____

12. _____

■ E. ANSWER *Answer these questions about your classmates using a quantifier.*

EXAMPLE

Q: Are all of the students in your class from the same country?

A: Many of us are from the Philippines. A few of us are from Mexico.

1. Are all of the students in your class from the same country?
2. Do all of the students in your class speak the same language?
3. Were all of the students in your class on time today?
4. Do all of the males in your class have dark hair?
5. Do all of the females in your class have long hair?
6. Do all of the students in your class do their homework?
7. Are any of the students in your room wearing baseball caps?
8. Are any of the students in your class engaged?
9. Do any of the students in your class have young children?
10. Do any of the men in your class wear an earring?

Working Together

■ A. THE GROUP *Sit in a group of five or six students. Find several similarities and differences among yourselves. Write ten sentences about your group, beginning with the phrases below. The expressions in the box will give you some ideas.*

Everyone   All of us

Someone   Most of us

No one   Many of us

Some of us

A few of us

A couple of us

One of us

None of us

| have a computer |
| take the bus to school |
| play tennis |
| go dancing every weekend |
| (be) intelligent |
| have a pet |

B. STUDENT TO STUDENT

Student A: *Turn to page 184. Read the eight sentences about the boxes to your partner.*

Student B: *Look at the picture below and listen to your partner read eight sentences. Circle* **True** *if the statement is true. Circle* **False** *if the statement is false.*

<table>
<tr><td>1.</td><td>True</td><td>False</td><td></td><td>5.</td><td>True</td><td>False</td></tr>
<tr><td>2.</td><td>True</td><td>False</td><td></td><td>6.</td><td>True</td><td>False</td></tr>
<tr><td>3.</td><td>True</td><td>False</td><td></td><td>7.</td><td>True</td><td>False</td></tr>
<tr><td>4.</td><td>True</td><td>False</td><td></td><td>8.</td><td>True</td><td>False</td></tr>
</table>

When you finish, **Student B** *will turn to page 184 and read eight new sentences about the boxes above.* **Student A** *will circle* **True** *or* **False.**

■ C. CLASSIFY *Add four animals to this list. Classify these animals and make sentences.*

| EXAMPLE |

Most of these animals have four legs.

One of these animals hops.

Some of these animals are pets.

horse	lion	whale	cat
tiger	elephant	dog	kangaroo
mouse	zebra	deer	bear
sheep	fox	giraffe	cow

| _____ | _____ | _____ | _____ |

◼ A. WHICH VERB? *Circle the correct verb in these sentences.*

1. Everyone **is are** present today.

2. Someone **is are** wearing perfume.

3. Everyone **knows know** the answer.

4. Everyone **has have** a book.

5. Someone **is are** at the door.

6. All of the students **is are** writing the answer.

7. Most of the students **understands understand** the assignment.

8. A few of the students **walks walk** to school.

9. One of the students **lives live** an hour from here.

10. None of the students **speaks speak** Swahili.

◼ B. SEVEN SISTERS *Write seven sentences about these sisters. Use the expressions in the box in your sentences.*

all of the girls
most of the girls
many of the girls
some of the girls
a few of the girls
a couple of the girls
one of the girls
none of the girls

■ C. CLASSIFY
Use your imagination to think about each group of words. Write two sentences about each one.

1. Texas   California   Alaska   New York   Nevada   (states)

2. Boston   Los Angeles   San Francisco   Houston   Chicago   (cities)
3. Bush   Washington   Lincoln   Kennedy   Nixon   (presidents)
4. Independence Day   The Lion King   Batman   Jurassic Park   (movies)
5. cheesecake   apple pie   chocolate cake   brownies   cookies   (desserts)
6. dogs   cats   birds   fish   hamsters   horses   (pets)
7. Yankees   Dodgers   Mets   Red Sox   Giants   Cubs   (baseball teams)

Having Fun with the Language

■ A. SURVEY
*Design a survey to give to another class in your school. It should concentrate on one topic, such as school, recreation, or music. Ask ten questions in which the answer is **Yes** or **No.** For example: Do you have a pet? Do you study in the library? Do you like rock music? Distribute the survey, ask the students to complete it, and then collect the survey papers. Write ten sentences about the other class according to the survey results.*

Grammar Summary

1. *Everyone, someone, anyone,* and *no one* are singular.

Everyone is present.
Someone is at the door.
No one is absent.
Is anyone from China? (Note: Use anyone for questions.)

2. Quantifiers

Quantifiers can be singular or plural. Refer to the noun.

All of the **students** are from Mexico.	This sentence is plural.
All of the **information** is in the almanac.	This sentence is singular.
One of the students is registering.	*One of the* is always singular.
None of the students **is** absent.	Both of these forms are correct for *none*.
None of the students **are** absent.	

Requests and Favors

Grammar in Action

A. LISTEN: REQUESTS *Listen to each request. Write the number of the request in the box next to each person's name.*

Requests
Can I borrow a dollar?
Could I borrow a dollar?

B. LISTEN AND WRITE *Listen to the speakers again and write each request.*

1. Can ___I get a drink of water_____? Wait until after class, please.

2. _____? Of course.

3. Could _____? Wait until break time, please.

4. _____? Yes, you can.

5. Could _____? Sure. Here.

C. REQUESTS *Read these sentences and make a request. Begin your request with* **Can I** *or* **Could I.**

> **EXAMPLE**
>
> **You want to look at your friend's book.**
>
> Can I look at your book, please?

1. You want to borrow your friend's eraser.
2. You want to use your friend's pencil.
3. You want to look at your friend's notebook.
4. You want to copy your friend's homework.
5. You want to borrow your friend's dictionary.
6. You want to use your friend's pencil sharpener.

D. I DON'T UNDERSTAND *Sometimes we don't understand what a person said or we need a person to explain something again. Repeat these sentences with* **Would you** *or* **Could you** *after your teacher.*

Favors
Would you help me?
Could you help me?

Would you	help me?
	spell that?
	explain that?
	say that again?
	repeat that?
Could you	speak more slowly?
	speak more loudly?

Read each situation on page 70 and use an expression from the box to ask for assistance.

> **EXAMPLE**
>
> Situation: You want someone to repeat an address.
>
> Request: Would you say that address again, please?

1. You want someone to repeat a telephone number.
2. Someone is talking very fast.
3. You need some help with your homework.
4. Someone is talking too softly.
5. You didn't understand an address.
6. You can't spell a new word.
7. You don't understand a sign.

Working Together

■ A. REQUESTS *Use these phrases and illustrations to make requests of a friend or family member.*

Can I   Would you

Could I   Could you

> **Borrow and Lend**
>
> Both *borrow* and *lend* mean to use temporarily. You plan to return the item.
>
> Can **I borrow** your tape? = Can I use your tape?
>
> Can **you lend** me your tape? = Can you give me your tape?

EXAMPLE

Could you drive me to school?

Can I borrow your car for an hour?

■ B. CAN I HAVE...? *Give another student everything on your desk. Then ask for each item until you have everything back again.*

EXAMPLE

Can I have my notebook?

Would you please return my pencils?

Could you give me back my glasses?

◼ A. COMPLETE *Begin each sentence with an expression from the box below. Choose an appropriate verb.*

Can I	Would you
Could I	Could you

look at	drive	lend
borrow	speak	help
translate	show	

1. _Could I_ _____ _borrow_ _____ $10 for gas? I'll pay you back tomorrow.
2. _____ _____ me to work? My car has a flat.
3. _____ _____ me how to use this computer program?
4. _____ _____ your dictionary to check the spelling of a word?
5. _____ _____ me move into my new apartment?
6. _____ _____ this letter for me? I don't speak Spanish.
7. _____ _____ me $100 for two days? I get paid on Friday.
8. Hello. _____ _____ to Mr. Johnson, please?

◼ B. SCHOOL SITUATIONS *Write a request or ask a favor for each situation.*

1. You are in the main office. You want to make a copy of your driver's license.
2. You are in class. Your pencil breaks.
3. You are at the public telephone with a friend. You don't have any change.
4. You are in the office. You want to see the director.
5. You are reading a story in class. You don't understand one of the words.
6. You were absent yesterday. You want the homework assignment.
7. You are in the office and need to call home.
8. You didn't do your homework. You want to bring the assignment tomorrow.

Grammar Summary

◼ 1. Can I or Could I *We make a request with Can I or Could I.*

Can I borrow an eraser?	Sure, you can.
Could I get a drink of water, please?	No, I'm sorry.

◼ 2. Would you or Could you *We ask a favor with Would you or Could you.*

Would you lend me a dollar?	Of course.
Could you help me with this?	No problem.

8 Plans and Predictions

Future Tense: *Going to* and *Will*

Grammar in Action

Future: *Going to*

A. LISTEN: FUTURE PLANS *Today is graduation at Central High School. Listen to each student's plans; then write his or her name under the correct picture.*

Brian   Alex   Dan   Diana
Lisa   Tom   Sally   Kelly

Future: *going to*		
I	am	
He		
She	is	
It		going to study.
We		
You	are	
They		

Repeat each student's plans. Use both formal and conversational pronunciation.

EXAMPLE

Formal: Dan is *going to* join the army.

Conversational: Dan is *gonna* join the army.

> Note: *gonna* is only used in speaking.
> We cannot use *gonna* in writing.

■ B. ALEX'S PLANS *Alex is graduating from high school today. His dream is to open a restaurant in San Francisco. Arrange his future plans in a logical order.*

_____ a. He's going to take cooking classes.

_____ b. He's going to expand his restaurant.

__1__ c. Alex is going to work as a waiter.

_____ d. He's going to work as a chef's assistant.

_____ e. He's going to open a small restaurant.

_____ f. He's going to borrow money from his older brother.

■ C. DIANA'S PLANS *Diana is graduating from high school today. She wants to become a registered nurse (RN), but she has enough money for only one year of school. Complete this paragraph about her plans.*

In September, Diana __is going to start__ (start) classes at the local community college. She _____ (study) to be a licensed practical nurse (LPN). The college has a one-year program. After she graduates, Diana _____ (work) full time for two or three years and save money. Then she _____ (go) back to school and study for her registered nurse license (RN).

■ D. FUTURE QUESTIONS *Complete these questions in the future tense about the students' plans. Use the verbs below.*

start   get   join   fly   take

> **Future Questions**
> Are you going to travel?
> Is she going to travel?
> Are they going to travel?

1. When __is__ Sally __going to get__ married? In August.

2. When _____ Kelly _____ to Europe? The day after tomorrow.

3. When _____ Lisa _____ to work? Next month.

4. When _____ Alex _____ cooking classes? In a few months.

5. When _____ Dan _____ the army? This summer.

Complete these questions about your plans. Use the verbs below.
Answer with a future time expression.

see   finish   pay   visit   take

Future Time Expressions
tomorrow
the day after tomorrow
this afternoon
this evening
next week
next summer
next year
in a few minutes
in a few days
in a little while
soon
later

1. When ___are___ we ___going to finish___ this class?

   _____

2. When _____ you _____ a vacation?

   _____

3. When _____ you _____ the doctor?

   _____

4. When _____ you _____ your telephone bill?

   _____

5. When _____ you _____ your friend?

   _____

Write two more questions using the future tense. Ask another student your questions.

Future: *Will*

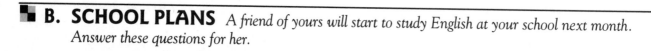

A. FUTURE PLANS *Discuss the plans of each of the students*
graduating from high school on page 72. Use the future tense
*with **will**.*

Future *will*

I		
He		
She		
It	will	study.
We	won't	
You		
They		

> **EXAMPLE**
>
> Brian will sign a contract with a baseball team.
>
> Sally will get married.

B. SCHOOL PLANS *A friend of yours will start to study English at your school next month.*
Answer these questions for her.

1. How much will I pay in tuition?
2. Will I need to buy books?
3. Will I have to take a test before I begin?
4. How many hours will I attend class each week?

5. How many hours will I need to study each day?

6. Will you help me with my English?

7. How long will it take me to learn English?

 C. I'LL HELP YOU *Make an offer to help in each of these situations.*
*Use the verb in parentheses and **it, him,** or **her** in your answer.*

> Use *will* to make
> an offer to help..

EXAMPLE

The telephone is ringing. (answer)   I'll answer **it.**

Susan needs a ride home. (take)   I'll take **her.**

1. This box is very heavy. (carry)

2. That light bulb is out. (change)

3. Susan doesn't understand her algebra homework. (help)

4. Where's Tom? He's late. (call)

5. The volume is too loud. (turn/down)

6. Mary needs a ride to school. (drive)

7. I can't reach that book on the top shelf. (get)

D. LISTEN: PRESENT AND PRESENT CONTINUOUS WITH FUTURE MEANING *The school newspaper is interviewing two graduating seniors about their future plans. Listen to the interviews; then answer the questions.*

> With definite future plans, especially those with a specific date or time, we can use the future, the present continuous or the present.
> I'm **going to leave** on Thursday.
> I'm **leaving** on Thursday.
> I **leave** on Thursday.

Sally   Dan

1. Is Dan going to go to college?

2. What is he going to do?

3. When does he leave for basic training?

4. How long is basic training?

5. When does he start technical training?

6. How long is he going to stay in the army?

7. When is Sally getting married?

8. Where are they going for their honeymoon?

9. Will she go to college full time?

10. Is she going to work?

11. Where is she going to work?

E. THE CENSUS: POPULATION CHANGES
The charts below illustrate the United States' changing population picture. The Census Bureau predicts a slow population growth, but one that will be increasingly more ethnically diverse. Study the charts and answer the questions.

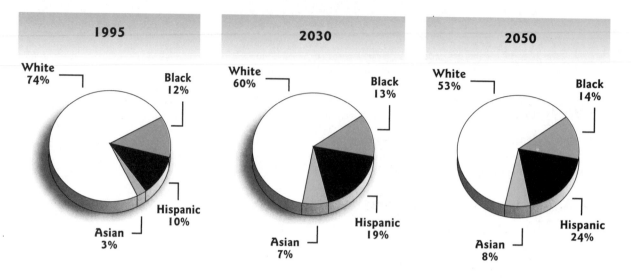

1995	2030	2050
White 74%	White 60%	White 53%
Black 12%	Black 13%	Black 14%
Hispanic 10%	Hispanic 19%	Hispanic 24%
Asian 3%	Asian 7%	Asian 8%

Note: Numbers do not add up to 100 because of American Indian population and rounding.

1995	2030	2050
Population: 264 million	Population: 340 million	Population: 400 million

Source: U.S. Bureau of the Census, 1995.

1. What was the population in 1995? Which ethnic group had the highest population? Which had the lowest?

2. What will the population be in 2030? In 2050?

3. According to the Census Bureau, which groups will grow the fastest? What do you think is the reason for their higher growth rate?

4. Which group will increase most slowly?

5. By the year 2050, the United States will be much more ethnically diverse than it is today. What changes will this bring in education? In language teaching? In supermarkets?

Working Together

A. INTERVIEW
*Sit in a group of three students. Ask these questions and write your partners' responses. Use **going to** or **will** in your answers.*

1. What are your plans for tomorrow?

_____

_____

2. What are your plans for next week?

_____

_____

3. What are your plans for next summer?

_____

_____

4. What are your plans for five years from now?

_____

_____

■ B. FIND SOMEONE WHO *Stand up and ask your classmates these questions about their plans for the next year. Try to find someone who answers* **Yes** *to each number. Write that student's name on the line.*

EXAMPLE

Are you going to change jobs?   No, I'm not. (Continue to ask other students.)

Are you going to change jobs?   Yes, I am. (Write that student's name.)

1. change jobs?   _____

2. move?   _____

3. visit your native country? _____

4. buy a house?   _____

5. get married?   _____

6. join an exercise club?   _____

7. get a driver's license?   _____

8. start a business?   _____

9. buy a computer?   _____

10. major in engineering?   _____

◼ C. FUTURE PREDICTIONS *Sit with a small group and read these predictions about the future.*
Decide if you Agree or Disagree with each one. Give your reasons.

	Agree	Disagree
1. Most people will live to be 100.		
2. There will be a cure for the common cold.		
3. Health care will be free.		
4. People will decide the sex of their children.		
5. Most cars will run on electricity.		
6. Most families will own a computer.		
7. Most homes will have a big-screen TV.		
8. Homes will order first-run movies. There will be fewer movie theaters.		

Sit in a group and discuss each topic below. Write one future prediction for each area.

Computers: _____

Jobs: _____

Politics: _____

Health: _____

Immigration: _____

D. STUDENT TO STUDENT *The chart below gives the future plans of four students.*
Ask and answer questions to complete the missing information.

Student A: *Look at the chart on page 79.*

Student B: *Turn to page 184.*

EXAMPLE

What is Yuri going to do?   He's going to travel.

Where is he going to travel?   In Europe.

	Jenny	Yuri	Amanda	Kevin
What		travel		open his own business
When	this summer		next month	
Where		in Europe		in Boston

Practicing on Your Own

A. FUTURE PLANS *Each situation describes what a person is doing now. Use your imagination and decide what each person **is going to** do or **will** do.*

1. Robert is buying two airline tickets.

   Robert is going to fly to Hawaii.

2. Samuel is opening a can of paint.

   _____

3. Sandra is wrapping a skirt and sweater.

   _____

4. Renata and Stanley are applying for visas.

   _____

5. John and Henry are packing their suitcases.

   _____

6. Linda is applying for a loan.

   _____

7. Paul is studying very hard.

   _____

8. Rick and Crystal are decorating their living room with signs and balloons.

   _____

9. Yoon is putting film in her camera.

   _____

10. Carl is putting on his pajamas.

   _____

B. TENSE CONTRAST *Complete these conversations with two seniors in college. Use the future, present continuous, or present tense.*

A: What _____are_____ you _____studying_____ (study) now?

B: Occupational therapy.

A: When _____ you _____ (graduate)?

B: Next month, in May.

A: Where _____ you _____ (look) for a job?

B: I already _____ (have) a job. I _____ (work) at Jackson

Center. It's a senior center.

A: _____ you _____ (graduate) in May?

B: Yes, I _____ . May 15th.

A: What _____ you _____ (do) after that?

B: I _____ (look) for a teaching job. My major is special education.

A: _____ you _____ (stay) in this area?

B: No, there aren't many jobs in Pennsylvania. I _____ (apply) in states

like New Mexico and Nevada. The population is really growing there.

A: Good luck. I'm sure you _____ (find) something.

C. PROMISES *Read these sentences; then make an offer or promise to help. Use **will** in your sentences.*

1. I don't know how to get to Austin.

   I'll give you directions. _____

2. It's hot in here.

   _____

3. The doorbell is ringing.

   _____

4. I'm really thirsty.

   _____

5. That music is too loud.

   _____

6. I don't have a ride home today.

   _____

7. I have a dentist appointment, but my baby-sitter just called and canceled.

   _____

8. I don't know how to fill out this form.

   _____

Sharing Our Stories

Read Patrick's story about his plans for the future.

I am studying English four nights a week. In the future, I'm planning to work in the field of telecommunications. When I was 18 years old, I got a certificate in telecommunications in Haiti. I learned how to be a receptionist and a telephone operator. When I finish my English courses, I'm going to look for a job. First, I'll look for a job with a local telephone company as an operator. If I'm successful, I'm going to look for a job in a larger company. Right now, I'm going to stay at the college where I study English and take more courses. In the future, maybe I'll transfer to another college. At one time, I thought about studying computers, but I don't like math. I'm going to find a program that doesn't require a lot of math, so I'm going to talk to a counselor again.

Patrick Fleurimond, Haiti

 What are your plans for the future? Choose one goal and describe it. How are you going to reach this goal? Describe your plans step by step.

◾ A. MAKING PREDICTIONS

Sit in a small group and choose a student. Make predictions about his or her future. Read some of your predictions.

1. I think you are going to study _____.

2. I think you will finish college in _____ (year).

3. I think you will be a _____.

4. I think you will move to _____ (state).

5. I think that you will take a trip to _____.

6. I think you will   **stay in this country**   **return to your country.**

7. I think you will _____.

Write two more predictions about this student.

_____

_____

◾ B. SCHOOL EVENTS

Several students should volunteer to look around the school at bulletin boards, posters, flyers, etc. Talk to the director of student activities, the sports office, or any other persons on your campus or at your school who are in charge of activities and events. Report to the class on some of the upcoming events and club meetings. Be sure to copy the date, time, and location. Make a list of some of the activities that interest you.

Grammar Summary

◾ I. Future: *Be + Going to*

Be + going to talks about actions and plans in the future.

I'm **going to begin** college in September.

He **isn't going to major** in science. He's **going to study** accounting.

2. *Yes/no questions*

	Short answers	
Am I **going to graduate?**	Yes, you are.	No, you aren't.
Are you **going to go** to college?	Yes, I am.	No, I'm not.
Is he **going to join** the army?	Yes, he is.	No, he isn't.
Is it **going to be** difficult?	Yes, it is.	No, it isn't.
Are we **going to travel?**	Yes, we are.	No, we aren't.
Are you **going to work?**	Yes, we are.	No, we aren't.
Are they **going to study?**	Yes, they are.	No, they aren't.

3. *Wh* questions

	Answers
When **am** I **going to graduate?**	Next year.
What **are** you **going to study?**	Engineering.
How long **is** she **going to wait?**	For a year.
Where **are** we **going to travel?**	To India.

4. Future: *Will*

Will talks about actions in the future.	He'll buy a car soon.
Will is often used for the immediate future.	I'll buy some milk on my way home.
Will expresses a promise or offer to help.	I'll help you move.
Will is used to make predictions.	She'll get the job.

5. *Yes/no questions*

	Short answers	
Will you **study** nursing?	Yes, I will.	No, I won't.
Will he **sign** a contract?	Yes, he will.	No, he won't.
Will they **get** married?	Yes, they will.	No, they won't.

6. *Wh* questions

	Answers
When **will** you **finish** this work?	Tomorrow morning.
Where **will** you **leave** the package?	In your mailbox.
Who **will be** the next president?	I don't know.

 **Cities**

Comparative Adjectives

■ **A. MY CITY** *Circle the correct information about the city where you live.*

1. The population in this city is **over 100,000** **under 100,000.**

2. Unemployment is **high** **moderate** **low.**

3. It is **easy** **difficult** to find a job.

84

4. Houses are **very expensive   expensive   affordable.**

5. Property taxes are **high   average   low.**

6. The state sales tax is _____ %.

7. This city is **very safe   safe   not very safe.**

8. In the summer, the weather is **warm   hot   very hot.** The average temperature is about _____ degrees.

9. In the winter, the weather is **warm   cool   cold   very cold.** The average temperature is about _____ degrees.

10. This area receives **a lot of rain   an average amount of rain   very little rain.**

11. The schools in this city are **excellent   good   fair   poor.**

◼ B. CLASSIFY *These adjectives are often used to describe a city or town. Write each adjective in the correct column.*

large	small	beautiful	friendly	safe
dangerous	quiet	convenient	good	low
busy	noisy	clean	affordable	interesting

One syllable	Two syllables ending with *y*	Two or more syllables, not ending with *y*
large	busy	dangerous

■ C. COMPARATIVE FORM
Study the examples. Write the comparative form of the adjectives below.

One syllable	Two syllables ending with *y*	Two or more syllables, not ending with *y*
large—larger than	busy—busier than	modern—more modern than
old—older than	noisy—noisier than	dangerous—more dangerous than
big—bigger than	dirty—dirtier than	convenient—more convenient than

clean   cleaner than _____   cold   _____

expensive   more expensive than _____   friendly   _____

sunny   sunnier than _____   good   _____

bad   _____   affordable   _____

beautiful   _____   windy   _____

warm   _____   safe   _____

interesting   _____   populated   _____

■ D. TWO CITIES
Complete each sentence below with the names of cities or towns in your area.

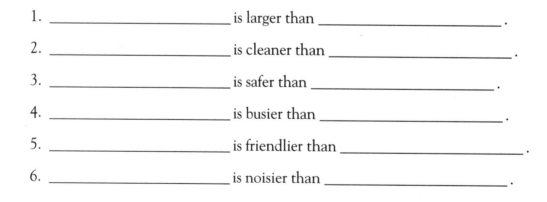

1. _____ is larger than _____.

2. _____ is cleaner than _____.

3. _____ is safer than _____.

4. _____ is busier than _____.

5. _____ is friendlier than _____.

6. _____ is noisier than _____.

■ E. COUNTRY FACTS

*Choose the appropriate adjective and compare your native country with the United States. Remember to use **than** where needed.*

_____ is _____ the U.S.
  (native country)   (large/small)

1. _____ is _____ the U.S.
     (native country)   (large/small)

2. In the summer, the weather in _____ is _____ in the U.S.
                                      (native country)   (hot/cool)

3. Food prices in _____ are _____ in the U.S.
                      (native country)   (high/low)

4. Public transportation in _____ is _____
                                (native country)   (convenient)
   in the U.S.

5. It is _____ to find a job in _____ than in the U.S.
            (easy/difficult)   (native country)

6. Going out at night is _____ in _____ than in the U.S.
                             (safe/dangerous)   (native country)

7. Housing prices in _____ are _____ in
                         (native country)   (expensive)
   the U.S.

Write two more sentences comparing life in your country with life in the United States.

_____

_____

F. LISTEN: THE BEST PLACES TO LIVE *Every year in its July issue, Money magazine rates the best places to live in the United States. In 1996, the top two cities were Madison, Wisconsin, and Punta Gorda, Florida. Find these two states on the map inside the back cover. Listen to the information about these cities and complete the chart below.*

	Madison, Wisconsin	Punta Gorda, Florida
Population		
Unemployment rate		
Cost of a three-bedroom house		
Property taxes		
State tax		
Schools		
Annual sunny days		
Average temperature	Summer: Winter:	Summer: Winter:

Use the information in your chart to write seven sentences comparing the two cities.

G. CITY FACTS *Read these facts about cities in the United States and make a statement with the adjective or phrase in parentheses.*

> **EXAMPLE**
>
> There are 23 symphony orchestras, four opera companies, two ballet companies, and five professional theaters in Boston. There is one symphony orchestra in Danbury, Connecticut. (cultural activities)
>
> There are **more cultural activities** in Boston than in Danbury.

1. The population of Portland, Oregon, is 497,000. The population of Omaha, Nebraska, is 336,000. (populated)

2. In Washington, D.C., you can travel by car, bus, train, or subway. In Ft. Lauderdale, Florida, you can travel by car or bus. (convenient)

3. The average humidity in Salt Lake City, Utah, is 55%. The average humidity in Olympia, Washington, is 78%. (humid)

4. In Denver, Colorado, there are 36 movie theaters, a zoo, three professional sports teams, and five parks. In Goldsboro, North Carolina, there are three movie theaters and one park. (interesting)

5. The average rent for a one-bedroom apartment in New York City is $750. The average rent for a one-bedroom apartment in Los Angeles is $800 per month. (expensive)

6. The average price for a three-bedroom home in Honolulu, Hawaii, is $310,000. The average price for a three-bedroom home in Ann Arbor, Michigan, is $104,000. (affordable)

7. The expected growth rate for jobs is 8% in Austin, Texas. The expected job growth rate is 2% in San Angelo, Texas. (job opportunities)

Working Together

■ A. WHAT'S IMPORTANT TO YOU? *In deciding where to live, these eight characteristics are important to Americans. Check the four most important characteristics for you. Explain your choices to your group.*

_____ low crime rate   _____ clean environment

_____ quality health care   _____ great schools

_____ low taxes   _____ strong job market

_____ affordable housing   _____ close to family

■ B. COMPARING NEIGHBORHOODS *Complete this information about your neighborhood by circling the correct information. Talk about your information with a partner and write five sentences comparing your neighborhoods.*

1. In my neighborhood, the people

    a. are very friendly.   b. just say "hello."   c. don't talk to each other.

2. The homes and apartments in my area are

    a. expensive.   b. reasonable.   c. inexpensive.

3. My neighborhood is

    a. pretty.   b. ordinary, but clean.   c. not very attractive.

4. The schools in my area are

    a. very good.   b. good.   c. not too good.

5. The streets in my area

    a. are quiet.   b. are usually quiet.   c. are noisy.

6. My neighborhood is

    a. safe.   b. usually safe.   c. dangerous.

C. STUDENT TO STUDENT *Your partner will read you ten questions about the two largest cities in the United States. Look at the chart below and circle the correct answer.*

Student A: *Turn to page 185.*
Student B: *Look at the information in the chart below. Listen and circle* **New York** *or* **Los Angeles**.

	New York	Los Angeles
Professional sports teams	7	6
Average household income	$67,201	$71,029
Average state and local taxes	$6,104	$4,421
Job growth expected	-1%	2.6%
Price of an average house	$237,000	$268,000
Average rent for a one-bedroom apartment	$725	$780
Number of colleges	18	24
Number of hospitals	79	124
Museums and art galleries	52	33
Annual rainfall	40 inches	12 inches
Average temperature (January)	38	65
Average temperature (July)	85	75

1. New York   Los Angeles
2. New York   Los Angeles
3. New York   Los Angeles
4. New York   Los Angeles
5. New York   Los Angeles

6. New York   Los Angeles
7. New York   Los Angeles
8. New York   Los Angeles
9. New York   Los Angeles
10. New York   Los Angeles

When you finish, **Student B** *will turn to page 185 and read ten new questions to* **Student A**.

■ D. MOVING
In a lifetime, the average American moves 11 times! In a small group, answer these questions about where Americans live and where they move.

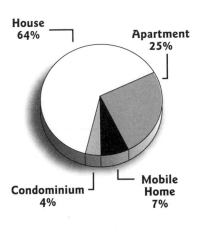

Do more people live in houses or in apartments?

What percentage of people rent?

Which are more popular, condos or mobile homes?

Are there many mobile homes in your area? Why or why not?

Condos are more popular in Florida than in any other state.

    What do you think is the reason?

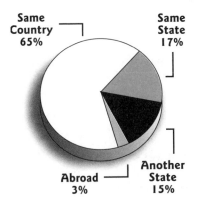

Do more people stay in the same state or move to a different state?

When people move, do they move near to or far from their home?

What percentage of people move to another state?

Why do you think Americans move so frequently?

In your native country, do people move frequently? Why or why not?

Source: U.S. Bureau of the Census, 1995.

Practicing on Your Own

■ A. ADJECTIVES
Read these sentences and circle the correct form of the adjective.

1. Denver, Colorado, is **higher**　**more higher**　than Tampa, Florida.

2. Mesa, Arizona, is growing　**faster**　**more faster**　than Philadelphia.

3. Los Angeles is　**humider**　**more humid**　than Midland, Texas.

4. Miami is **sunnier**   **more sunny**   than Seattle.

5. Dallas is **moderner**   **more modern**   than Philadelphia.

6. New York is **excitinger**   **more exciting**   than Kansas City.

7. Chicago is **crowdeder**   **more crowded**   than Tucson, Arizona.

8. Buffalo, New York, is **colder**   **more colder**   than Richmond, Virginia.

■ B. STATE FACTS *Write the comparative form of the adjective in parentheses.*

1. Rhode Island is _____ any other state. (small)

2. New Jersey is _____ any other state. (crowded)

3. Maryland is _____ any other state. (narrow)

4. Nevada is growing _____ any other state. (fast)

5. Oklahoma has a _____ number of Native Americans than any

   other state. (large)

6. Colorado is _____ any other state. (high)

7. Louisiana is _____ any other state. (wet)

8. California is _____ any other state. (populated)

■ C. TWO CITIES *Read these descriptions of Chicago and Houston.*

Chicago, Illinois, is the third largest city in the United States. It is in the northeastern corner of the state, on Lake Michigan. Chicago is warm in the summer but very cold in the winter. A strong wind blows off Lake Michigan year round.

Chicago has about 2,800,000 people. It is a major industrial and cultural center. Many businesses have their offices in the downtown area. Famous skyscrapers include the Sears Tower and the John Hancock Building. There are more than twenty colleges and universities in the city. Chicago also offers a symphony orchestra, many art museums, international restaurants, parks, beaches, sports arenas, and a zoo.

Houston, Texas, is the fourth largest city in the United States. It is in the southeastern part of the state, on the Gulf of Mexico. Houston is hot and sunny. In the summer, the average temperature is 90°. In the winter, it is 68°.

Houston has a population of 1,700,000 people. This large, modern city is a center of the oil industry. Houston is a port city; it ships cotton, oil, steel, and chemicals to many parts of the world. There are several large universities in Houston. Additionally, Houston has a symphony orchestra, several art museums, parks, and the huge Houston Astrodome for sports.

*Ask questions with **Which** about the two cities; then write the answer.*

1. (large)   Which city is larger? _____   Chicago is. _____

2. (modern)   _____   _____

3. (cold)   _____   _____

4. (windy)   _____   _____

5. (populated) _____   _____

6. (old)   _____   _____

7. (interesting) _____   _____

Sharing Our Stories

Read Steven's story about Hong Kong.

Hong Kong is a peninsula located on the southeastern coast of China.

The standard of living is very high in Hong Kong. A married couple usually lives with the extended family since it's very expensive to buy an apartment. For example, a 650-square-foot two-bedroom, one-bathroom apartment in Kowloon will cost approximately $180,000 U.S. dollars. This apartment can accommodate five people. Since space is so limited, the living room will be turned into an additional bedroom at night with a folding bed. Food, on the other hand, is very inexpensive. A nice sit-down dinner for a family of five will cost approximately $25 U.S. dollars.

The subway transportation is convenient and clean. Subway tokens are not used. Instead of tokens, people use a magnetic card, which you can purchase in denominations of $10, $50, or $100. The system automatically deducts the correct fare as you slide your card through a machine when entering and exiting.

Steven Lee, Hong Kong

Write about your hometown or your country. Where is it? How is the economy? Is it expensive to live there? Talk about everyday life, concentrating on two or three areas, such as homes, recreational and cultural activities, transportation, the weather, or job opportunities. Give specific details.

◼ A. MY CLASSMATE AND I

Sit with a partner. Talk about yourselves and then write five sentences using comparative adjectives. These questions may help you:

How tall are you?

How many children (or brothers and sisters) do you have?

How far do you live from school?

How many hours do you study?

◼ B. PICTURES

Cut out several pictures of athletes or sports events from a newspaper or a magazine. Compare two sports or two athletes who play the same sport.

◼ C. THE BEST PLACES TO LIVE

Find the most recent July issue of Money magazine in the library. Which two cities does this magazine rate as the top cities this year? Find them on a map of the United States. What reasons does the magazine give for the ratings? Is the city you live in one of the top ten best cities to live? Why or why not?

Grammar Summary—Comparative Adjectives

1. Comparative adjectives *To compare two people or things, use the comparative form of the adjective:*

New York is **larger than** Denver.

An apartment in New York is **more expensive than** an apartment in Denver.

Adjective	Form
1. One-syllable adjectives	Add **r** or **er** + *than.*
old →	older than
large	larger than
big	bigger than
Note: If an adjective ends with a consonant, vowel, consonant, then double the final consonant: big—bigger.	
2. Two-syllable adjectives that end with **y**	Change the **y** to **i** and add **er** + *than.*
busy →	busier than
noisy	noisier than
3. Adjectives with two or more syllables	Use **more** + *than.*
interesting →	more interesting
beautiful	more beautiful

2. Irregulars

good	better
bad	worse
far	farther
	more
	less

 **10 Learning English**

Can

 A. LISTEN: LEARNING ENGLISH *Gloria began to study English two months ago. Listen to her speak about herself and about learning to speak English; then circle* **can** *or* **can't** *in each sentence.*

1. Gloria   can   (can't)   speak English well.

2. She   can   can't   speak English with her neighbors.

3. Gloria   can   can't   watch TV in Spanish.

4. She   can   can't   speak Spanish at the store.

5. She   can   can't   use a Spanish-speaking bank teller.

6. Gloria   can   can't   understand the teacher.

7. She   can   can't   read her English book.

8. She   can   can't   follow people when they speak quickly.

9. Gloria   can   can't   ask questions easily in English.

10. She   can   can't   practice English with her children.

Can—Can't		
I You He She It We They	can can't	speak English

◼ B. QUESTIONS ABOUT ENGLISH *Ask and answer these questions about Gloria's English and about your English.*

EXAMPLE

Can Gloria speak English?

Yes, she can.

No, she can't.

Can you speak English?

Yes, I can.

No, I can't.

Yes/No Questions		
Can	I you he she we they	understand? read English?

1. Can Gloria speak Spanish?

2. Can Gloria speak English fluently?

3. Can Gloria ask questions in English?

4. Can Gloria speak English on the phone?

5. Can Gloria practice English in her neighborhood?

6. Can Gloria practice English with her children?

7. Can you speak Spanish?

8. Can you speak English fluently?

9. Can you ask questions in English?

10. Can you speak English on the phone?

11. Can you practice English in your neighborhood?

12. Can you practice English with your children?

C. LISTEN: PRONUNCIATION

*Listen to these sentences about Gloria and her children. Circle **can** or **can't**. Then read the sentences to a partner.*

1. Gloria's children   **can**   **can't**   speak English.

2. They   **can**   **can't**   speak Spanish, too.

3. Her son   **can**   **can't**   read Spanish.

4. Her daughter   **can**   **can't**   read Spanish.

5. She   **can**   **can't**   only read English.

6. Gloria   **can**   **can't**   speak English with her children.

7. She   **can**   **can't**   speak with their teachers, either.

8. She   **can**   **can't**   help them with their homework.

> Note the difference in the sound of **a**.
> They can speak English.
> They can't speak English.

D. MY NATIVE LANGUAGE

*Gloria lives in a Spanish-speaking neighborhood. She speaks Spanish with her friends and others in her community. Read each statement; then talk about **your** situation.*

1. Gloria can rent Spanish videos. Can you rent videos in your native language?

2. Gloria can buy Spanish food at the local supermarket. Can you buy food from your country at the local supermarket?

3. Gloria can eat in Spanish restaurants. Can you eat your native food in restaurants in your neighborhood?

4. Gloria can listen to the news in Spanish. Can you listen to the news in your language?

5. Gloria can talk to her neighbors in Spanish. Can you talk to your neighbors in your native language?

6. Gloria can read the Spanish language newspaper. Can you get the newspaper in your native language?

7. Gloria can celebrate several Spanish holidays with her neighbors because most of them are Hispanic. Can you celebrate your native holidays with your neighbors?

8. Gloria can watch Spanish language TV. Can you watch any TV programs in your native language?

Working Together

A. MY ENGLISH
Complete each sentence about your English. Then listen to your partner read his or her sentences. Circle the correct information about your partner.

My Partner

1. I _____ understand the teacher.

2. I _____ follow people when they speak slowly.

3. I _____ understand TV in English.

4. I _____ understand some American songs.

5. I _____ read traffic signs in English.

6. I _____ speak English at the store.

7. I _____ speak English with my family.

8. I _____ speak English on the telephone.

9. I _____ read the newspaper in English.

10. I _____ understand the weather report on the radio.

11. I _____ speak English with my classmates.

12. I _____ follow a conversation between two Americans.

1. can   can't

2. can   can't

3. can   can't

4. can   can't

5. can   can't

6. can   can't

7. can   can't

8. can   can't

9. can   can't

10. can   can't

11. can   can't

12. can   can't

What are two things you both can do? What are two things that are difficult for both of you?

B. GETTING MORE PRACTICE
*In a small group, discuss how you can get **more** practice listening to and speaking English. Check the suggestions that you think are helpful for **you.***

❏ I can watch TV in English.

❏ I can talk to my American neighbors or to American students.

❏ I can read the newspaper in English.

❏ I can watch the English lessons on local TV.

❏ I can volunteer at a food pantry, day care center, or other community service.

*Discuss other ways to practice your English. Write three of the suggestions that you think are helpful for **you.***

A. COMPLETE *Complete these sentences about your English. Use* **can** *or* **can't** *and one of the verbs below.*

order   understand   practice
speak   apply   ask
read

1. I _____ English on the telephone.

2. I _____ English with my family.

3. I _____ the newspaper in English.

4. I _____ for a job in English.

5. I _____ the commercials in English on TV.

6. I _____ English with my neighbors.

7. I _____ a pizza in English.

8. I _____ questions in English.

9. I _____ English when a person speaks slowly.

10. I _____ food in English in a restaurant.

B. QUESTIONS WITH CAN *Look at this information about English classes at a private school. Ask and answer questions with* **can** *and the verbs on page 101.*

English Language Classes

Classes: Beginning, Intermediate, and Advanced

Cost: $200 per 6-week session

Classes available: Monday and Wednesday   9:00 A.M. to 11:00 A.M.

                       Tuesday and Thursday   7:00 P.M. to 9:00 P.M.

                       Saturday   9:00 A.M. to 1:00 P.M.

Extra help available in our English computer laboratory

Financial aid available

Additional courses: Pronunciation, TOEFL Preparation, Citizenship

---

study   take   use   apply

1. __Can___ a student __take__ classes in the morning?   __Yes, he can.__

2. _____ a student _____ classes in the afternoon?   _____

3. _____ a student _____ classes in the evening?   _____

4. _____ a student _____ here for free?   _____

5. _____ a student _____ for financial aid?   _____

6. _____ a student _____ a course in pronunciation?   _____

7. _____ a student _____ mathematics here?   _____

8. _____ a student _____ the computer lab?   _____

9. _____ a student _____ courses on Saturday?   _____

Having Fun with the Language

A. MY SKILLS *You can speak English. What other skills do you have? List at least five other things you can do. Talk about some things that you can't do but would like to do in the future.*

> **EXAMPLE**
>
> I **can make** delicious Chinese food.
>
> I **can play** the guitar.
>
> I **can't** swim, but I would like to learn!

Grammar Summary

I. *Can*

Can shows ability, skill, or know-how. It refers to present or future time.

Note: Do not use **s** with the third person singular.

I can speak English on the telephone.

She can speak English on the telephone.

I can't speak English on the telephone.

 **Marriage**

Have to/Don't have to/Should

Have to/Don't have to

A. LISTEN: WEDDING PLANS

Michael and Patty just got engaged. It's January, and they plan to get married in August. Listen to the timetable for some of their plans, and match the month and the item.

	Have to
	Have to shows necessity or obligation.
	I **have to** order the invitations.
	She **has to** order the invitations.
	They **have to** order the invitations.

__5__ January   1. Select the rings.

_____ February   2. Order the invitations.

_____ March   3. Pick out a wedding gown.

_____ April   4. Have blood tests and get the marriage license.

_____ May   5. Talk to their minister.

_____ June   6. Choose a place for the reception.

_____ July   7. Review all the arrangements.

_____ August   8. Send the invitations.

What do they have to do each month?

B. DON'T HAVE TO—DOESN'T HAVE TO

Patty and Michael have a helpful family who will be able to save them time and money on the wedding. What are some things that Patty and Michael **don't have to** *do or worry about? Use the phrases below to help you.*

❏ rent a tuxedo
❏ order a wedding cake
❏ look for an apartment
☑ hire a photographer
❏ rent a limousine
❏ draw a map for the guests

❏ worry about the weather
❏ change Patty's driver's license
❏ contact guests who did not respond
❏ make hotel reservations
❏ choose a dress

EXAMPLE

Michael's cousin is a professional photographer.
They **don't have to** hire a photographer.

	(Not) have to
	(Not) have to shows that an action is not necessary.
	I **don't have to** rent a tuxedo.
	He **doesn't have to** rent a tuxedo.
	They **don't have to** rent a tuxedo.

1. Patty's uncle owns a limousine service.
2. Everyone knows where the church is.
3. Patty's sister is going to bake the wedding cake.
4. Patty's is going to wear her mother's wedding gown.
5. They are going to live in Michael's apartment.
6. They are going to get married inside.
7. Everyone from both families lives less than an hour from the reception location.
8. Michael already owns a tuxedo.
9. Everyone responded to the wedding invitations.
10. Patty isn't going to take her husband's last name.

■ C. COMPARING CUSTOMS *Read each sentence about an American wedding. Compare it to the custom in your country.*

> **EXAMPLE**
>
> The bride and groom have to have blood tests.
> In Poland, the bride and groom have to have blood tests, too.   *or*
> In Poland, the bride and groom don't have to have blood tests.

1. The bride and groom have to have blood tests.
2. They have to get a marriage license from City Hall.
3. The couple has to reserve the church or temple many months before the wedding.
4. The couple doesn't have to get married in a church or temple.
5. Two people have to witness the marriage ceremony.
6. The bride doesn't have to wear white.
7. Each guest has to send or bring a gift.
8. The bride usually takes her husband's name, but she doesn't have to.

Should

A. LISTEN: DECISIONS, DECISIONS

Patty and Michael have a lot to decide about their wedding and reception. Listen to their conversation and answer these questions.

> **Should**
> *Should* expresses advice or an opinion.
> You **should** have a small wedding.
> She **should** have a small wedding.

1. Are they going to have a small wedding or a big wedding?
2. When are they going to get married?
3. Are they going to get married inside or outside?
4. Are they going to have the wedding and reception in the same location?
5. Where are they going to get married? Why?
6. Where are they going to have the reception? Why?

■ B. CONVERSATION *Complete these sentences from the conversation with **should** and one of the verbs below.*

get   look   invite   have

1. Maybe we __should__ just __invite__ brothers and sisters, aunts and uncles.

2. When _____ we _____ married, this spring or this summer?

3. _____ we _____ the wedding ceremony and the reception in the same place?

4. For the reception, maybe we _____ _____ for a place in the middle.

■ C. WHAT SHOULD THEY DO? *Patty and Michael are making decisions about the wedding and reception. Using **should**, give your opinion and a reason for each point below.*

A disc jockey costs about $300. A five-piece band is about $1,000. What should they do?

Opinion 1: They **should** hire a disc jockey. A DJ is much cheaper.

Opinion 2: They **should** hire a band. It's more fun to dance to live music.

1. Michael wants an all-white wedding cake. Patty wants an all-chocolate one.

2. Michael's cousin is a good photographer. Patty is nervous about using Michael's cousin. She wants to hire a professional photographer.

3. Patty wants an afternoon wedding and reception. Michael prefers an evening wedding and reception.

4. There will be about 200 people at the reception. A buffet dinner is less expensive than a sit-down dinner, but Patty and Michael don't want people standing in long lines.

5. Patty has brown hair. She's thinking about dying her hair much lighter for the wedding.

6. Michael has two brothers and can't decide which to ask to be his best man. He's closer to his younger brother, but he doesn't want to hurt his older brother's feelings.

7. Patty wants five bridesmaids, but she has two sisters and Michael has three sisters. She also wants her best friend, Emily, to be a bridesmaid.

Working Together

■ A. THE GUEST LIST *Michael is trying to limit his half of the guest list to 100 people. Does Michael need to invite all these people? Use **should, shouldn't, have to** and **don't have to** in your discussion.*

Parents (2)

Grandparents (4)

Brothers and sisters and their spouses and children (18)

Aunts and uncles (12)

First cousins (14)

Second cousins (18)

Boss and spouse (2)

Eight co-workers and one guest each (16)

Teacher at night school and guest (2)

Closest friends with guests (14)

Parents' best friends (14)

B. PACKING
Patty and Michael are deciding what to take on their honeymoon to Italy. Draw a box around each item they **have to take.** *Circle each item that they* **should take.** *Cross out each item that they* **don't have to take.**

passport	sun block	a laptop computer
~~a pillow~~	swimsuits	a bilingual dictionary
(sneakers)	laundry detergent	Patty's allergy medicine
health insurance card	aspirin	plane tickets
car keys	10 pairs of shoes	sunglasses
Michael's contact lenses	a camera	money

C. STUDENT TO STUDENT

Student A: *Read the four sentences on page 185 about marriage.*
Student B: *Listen and write each sentence under* **I agree** *or* **I disagree.**

I agree	I disagree

When you finish, change pages. **Student B** *will turn to page 185 and read four new sentences to* **Student A.**

D. THE AVERAGE WEDDING
The cost of an average wedding ranges from $15,000 to $20,000 and includes 188 guests. With a small group, answer these questions about the chart.

1. What is the most expensive part of the wedding?

2. Which expenses are not typical in your country? What are some additional expenses in your country?

3. What does an average photographer charge for a wedding?

Some Typical Wedding Expenses	
Reception	$7,000
Ring	3,000
Photographer	1,088
Flowers	863
Gown	852

4. Which of these expenses seem high to you?

5. How could you reduce the expense of a wedding?

Practicing on Your Own

■ **A. THE LEGALITIES** *Read this information about obtaining a marriage license. Underline* **have to, has to,** *and* **must.** *What other expressions show obligation?*

(Not) have to
(Not) have to shows that an action is not necessary.
I **don't have to** rent a tuxedo.
He **doesn't have to** rent a tuxedo.
They **don't have to** rent a tuxedo.

By law, all states require a marriage license. In order to obtain the license, the man and woman <u>must</u> present proof of age in the form of a birth certificate, immigration records, or a passport. Marriage age varies from state to state, but if the couple is under age, parental consent is needed. If either person was married before, that person has to bring his or her divorce decree. All states have a short waiting period before the wedding, usually two or three days. Finally, both the man and the woman have to present the results of a blood test. The cost for a marriage license is about $30. A minister, priest, rabbi, or justice of the peace performs the ceremony and two witnesses must be present. Traditionally, women take their husband's family name, but this custom is changing. Some women keep their family names, or they hyphenate their last name followed by their husband's. For example, if Susan Watson marries Richard Green, she can keep the name Susan Watson or take the name Susan Watson-Green.

Complete these statements about the legalities of marriage.

have to	must	don't have to
has to		doesn't have to

1. The couple to be married _____has to_____ obtain a marriage license.

2. The man and the woman _____ show proof of age.

3. They _____ show a birth certificate; a passport or immigration record is also acceptable.

4. The couple _____ wait a long time before they can marry.

5. Each person _____ present the results of a blood test.

6. A clergy member _____ perform the ceremony; a justice of the peace can perform it.

7. A woman _____ take her husband's name.

■ B. SHOULD *Use should and give your opinion about each situation.*

1. The wedding is next month. Patty has gained seven pounds, and her wedding gown is a little tight.

   Patty should relax and let out her wedding gown.

2. Patty wants the wedding on Saturday. Michael wants the wedding on Sunday.

   _____

3. Patty and Michael received three toaster ovens as gifts.

   _____

4. Patty wants to hire someone to take a video of the wedding. Michael thinks this is an unnecessary expense.

   _____

5. It's one week before the wedding, and Patty and Michael did not receive responses from five guests.

   _____

6. Patty wants her father to wear a tuxedo. Her father wants to wear his black suit.

   _____

7. Patty's mother wants to wear a big hat. Patty does not think this is appropriate.

   _____

■ C. MODAL CONTRAST *Complete each sentence with one of these modals.*

should	have to	don't have to
shouldn't	has to	doesn't have to
	must	

1. Pink is a pretty color. Patty ___should___ choose pink for the tablecloths and flowers.

2. Patty and Michael _____ coordinate a date that the church is available with a date that the reception hall is free.

3. Two people _____ witness a marriage.

4. Patty _____ buy white shoes because she already has a beautiful white pair.

5. The bridesmaids _____ select long dresses; short dresses are becoming more popular, especially for daytime weddings.

6. Michael's brother heard a good disc jockey last week. He thinks Michael _____ hire him for the wedding.

7. Patty and Michael _____ have blood tests.

8. Patty and Michael _____ buy a lot of furniture because Michael already has living room and kitchen furniture.

9. Michael _____ carry the wedding ring in his pocket. That's the best man's responsibility.

10. Guests _____ respond to their invitations shortly after receiving them.

■ D. FUTURE REVIEW *Life changes after marriage. Read this information about Patty and Michael and their lives now. Make predictions about the future using* **going to** *or* **will.**

1. Patty and Michael live in an apartment.
   <u>They will buy a house.</u>

2. Patty and Michael don't have any children.
   _____

3. They both work.
   _____

4. They live in the city.
   _____

5. They have two cars, a sports car and a small economy car.
   _____

6. Patty and Michael take lots of vacations.
   _____

7. They have lots of free time.
   _____

8. They have two salaries and can save money.
   _____

9. They go out to dinner three times a week.
   _____

10. Write one more prediction about Patty and Michael's future.
    _____

■ *Read Mery's story about her wedding in Iran.*

Mery Asgari is from Iran. She is married to Kazem Saifi, and they got married thirty years ago. Before she met Kazem, many other men had proposed to Mery, but she was picky and turned them all down.

Mery was on a holiday when she first saw her husband. It was the Shah's birthday, and she went to a celebration in another city. A man was there with his family. She began to smile at him. He looked at her and followed her around the party the rest of the day. Mery asked her sister-in-law about the man and decided she wanted to meet him.

Later, Kazem sent his parents to Mery's house in Tehran. At first, Mery's father said that they couldn't meet. Mery didn't know him well. So, Mery's father decided to find out more about Kazem. Mery's mother talked to people and found out that Kazem's family was respectable. They agreed to get married.

At that time in Iran, the groom's family usually had to pay for everything for the wedding. The bride had to bring everything for the home. Mery and Kazem spent a lot of time shopping. They had to spend one day shopping with family and friends. They spent a second day shopping for jewelry with close family members. They spent one day at the beauty salon for all the close members of the family. They spent a day at home and served everyone lunch and dinner. The bride spent one day with her family and friends, while the groom spent one day with his family and friends.

The night before the wedding, the groom's family came to Mery's home in a line of cars. They transported all the gifts for the wedding on the cars. The wedding dress was on a mannequin. The celebration lasted for seven days! Mery and Kazem's wedding was famous in their city because they were both from very respected families and Kazem was the oldest son.

Mery Asgari as told to Elizabeth Neblett

Write about a wedding ceremony and reception in your country. What do the bride and groom wear? Who attends? What are some of the wedding customs?

■ A. THE KEYS TO A GOOD MARRIAGE *What makes a good marriage? Sit with a group and decide on ten keys to a strong, loving marriage.*

You should each give 100% to the marriage.

You should listen to each other's opinions.

You should share the housework.

You should take time to enjoy yourselves.

Grammar Summary

■ I. *Have to/has to*

Have to expresses obligation or necessity. The obligation may be required by law, or it may be personal:

My sister **has to** get her marriage license soon.

I **have to** buy a gift for my sister's wedding.

■ 2. *Must*

Must also expresses obligation or necessity. *Must* is more formal and generally refers to laws and regulations:

You **must** show proof of age.

Two witnesses ***must*** sign the marriage license.

■ 3. *Don't have to/doesn't have to*

Don't have to shows that an action is not necessary:

I **don't have to** choose a gift because I'm going to give them a check.

Patty **doesn't have to** buy a dress because she's going to wear her mother's wedding dress.

■ 4. *Should*

Should expresses opinion or advice:

You **should** get married on a Sunday because more people are off from work that day.

You **shouldn't** get married at home. It's too much work.

12 Consumer Buying

Superlative Adjectives

 A. LISTEN: WHICH CAR? *Listen to the questions and check the answers.*

$25,000

$30,000

$12,000

1. ❑ a minivan	❑ a sports utility vehicle	❑ a subcompact
2. ❑ a minivan	❑ a sports utility vehicle	❑ a subcompact
3. ❑ a minivan	❑ a sports utility vehicle	❑ a subcompact
4. ❑ a minivan	❑ a sports utility vehicle	❑ a subcompact
5. ❑ a minivan	❑ a sports utility vehicle	❑ a subcompact
6. ❑ a minivan	❑ a sports utility vehicle	❑ a subcompact
7. ❑ a minivan	❑ a sports utility vehicle	❑ a subcompact
8. ❑ a minivan	❑ a sports utility vehicle	❑ a subcompact
9. ❑ a minivan	❑ a sports utility vehicle	❑ a subcompact
10. ❑ a minivan	❑ a sports utility vehicle	❑ a subcompact

◼ B. CURRENT MODELS
Tell your teacher the names of five popular cars to write on the black-board. Compare the cars by completing each sentence with the name of one of the cars.

1. The _____ is the largest.

2. The _____ is the fastest.

3. The _____ is the cheapest.

4. The _____ can carry the most passengers.

5. The _____ is the most expensive.

6. The _____ is the most economical to operate.

7. The _____ has the most powerful engine.

◼ C. CLASSIFY
Repeat each of the adjectives after your teacher and then write each adjective in the correct column.

fast	easy	beautiful	friendly
noisy	quiet	effective	good
economical	ugly	clean	affordable

One Syllable	Two Syllables Ending with *y*	Two or More Syllables, Not Ending with *y*
fast	noisy	economical

■ D. SUPERLATIVE FORM   *Study the examples.*
Write the superlatives of the adjectives below.

One Syllable	Two Syllables Ending with y	Two or More Syllables, Not Ending with y
large—the largest	noisy—the noisiest	economical—the most economical
old—the oldest	pretty—the prettiest	dangerous—the most dangerous
big—the biggest	dirty—the dirtiest	convenient—the most convenient

clean	the cleanest	cheap	_____
powerful	the most powerful	far	_____
difficult	_____	good	_____
bad	_____	affordable	_____
beautiful	_____	busy	_____
easy	_____	safe	_____
expensive	_____	comfortable	_____

■ E. CONTRAST   *Complete these sentences about the different types of cars. Be careful; some are comparative, and some are superlative.*

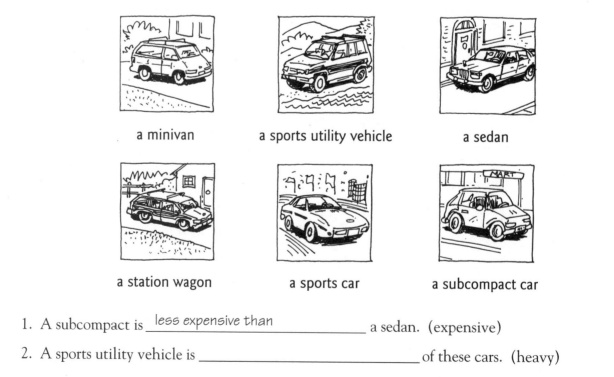

a minivan   a sports utility vehicle   a sedan

a station wagon   a sports car   a subcompact car

1. A subcompact is <u>less expensive than</u> _____ a sedan. (expensive)

2. A sports utility vehicle is _____ of these cars. (heavy)

114

3. A van is _____ of these cars for a large family. (convenient)

4. A subcompact car gets _____ gas mileage of any car. (good)

5. A sports car is _____ a van. (fast)

6. A sports utility vehicle with four-wheel drive is _____ in snow

than a sedan. (safe)

7. A sedan is _____ a sports utility vehicle. (quiet)

8. A subcompact car is _____ of all these cars. (economical)

9. A sports car is _____ a van. (comfortable)

10. A sports utility vehicle has _____ engine of these cars. (powerful)

Working Together

■ A. BRAND NAMES *Sit in a small group. Name three popular brands for each of these products.*
Use the adjectives below each group of products and compare them.

EXAMPLE

Student A: I think (brand-name) aspirin is the safest of the three.

Student B: I don't agree. I think (brand-name) aspirin is the safest.

1.

safe   effective   gentle to your stomach

2.

comfortable   cheap   popular

3.

effective   pleasant tasting

4.

strong   delicious

■ B. FAVORITE PRODUCTS *In a small group, talk about the products that you buy and use in your home. Write your product choice in each sentence and write the correct form of the adjective.*

1. _____ is _____ dishwashing liquid.
   (effective)

2. _____ is _____ soda.
   (refreshing)

3. _____ cream makes my skin feel _____ .
   (soft)

4. _____ orange juice is _____ .
   (fresh)

5. _____ detergent gets my clothes _____ .
   (clean)

6. _____ fabric softener gets my clothes _____ .
   (soft)

7. _____ rice is _____ .
   (delicious)

◼ C. INTERVIEW—CARS
Sit in a group of three students and answer these questions about your car or your family car. Then compare your cars and write one sentence about each fact from the chart.

EXAMPLE

My car is older than your car.

My car is the oldest of all.

Student:	1	2	3
1. What year is your car?			
2. How many miles does it have?			
3. How many miles does it get per gallon?			
4. How comfortable is the ride?			
5. How often does your car need repairs?			
6. Is it quiet, a little noisy, or noisy?			

Practicing on Your Own

◼ A. FOOD COMPARISONS
Write the superlative form of the adjective in parentheses.

1. Chicken is ___the healthiest___ meat for your heart. (healthy)

2. Vanilla is _____ flavor ice cream. (popular)

3. Pineapples are _____ fruit. (sweet)

4. Indian food is _____ kind of food. (spicy)

5. Watermelons are _____ fruit you can buy. (juicy)

6. Cheesecake is _____ dessert in this bakery. (heavy)

7. Pretzels are one of _____ snacks. (salty)

8. When you're thirsty, iced tea is one of _____ drinks you can have. (satisfying)

9. Thanksgiving dinner is _____ meal of the year. (long)

10. A sandwich is _____ food to bring for lunch. (easy)

■ B. THREE TV SETS
Americans love TV sets and buy 27 million sets a year. All three of these TV sets offer excellent quality and various features. Compare the TVs with the adjectives below.

	RCA	Panasonic	Mitsubishi
screen	35"	31"	27"
warranty	parts—1 year labor—90 days	parts—1 year labor—90 days tube—2 years	parts—1 year labor—1 year tube—2 years
weight	200 pounds	122 pounds	92 pounds
price	$1,800	$1,200	$950
picture	very good	outstanding	excellent

1. (small)   The Mitsubishi has the smallest screen. _____

2. (wide) _____

3. (short warranty) _____

4. (heavy) _____

5. (light) _____

6. (expensive) _____

7. (cheap) _____

8. (good picture) _____

■ C. GETTING THE FACTS
Look at each set of facts; then write a comparative and a superlative sentence about each group.

Big Companies
1. General Motors
2. Ford Motor
3. Exxon
4. Wal-Mart
5. AT&T

1. Exxon is bigger than AT&T.

2. General Motors is the biggest company.

Popular Snacks
1. Potato chips
2. Tortilla chips
3. Nuts
4. Pretzels
5. Popcorn

Large Fast-Food Chains
1. McDonald's
2. KFC (Kentucky Fried Chicken)
3. Burger King
4. Pizza Hut
5. Wendy's

Stressful Jobs
1. Firefighter
2. Race car drivers
3. Astronaut
4. Surgeon
5. Football player

Busy Airports
1. Atlanta
2. Chicago O'Hare
3. Dallas/Fort Worth
4. Los Angeles
5. Denver

Having Fun with the Language

■ A. OUR CLASS *Sit in a small group of three or four students. Use the adjectives in the list below and compare the students in your class.*

friendly	loud	arrives <u>late</u>
tall	studious	arrives <u>early</u>
young	talkative	athletic
quiet	<u>neat</u> handwriting	lives <u>far</u> from school
serious	<u>sloppy</u> handwriting	lives <u>close</u> to school

■ B. BE A SMART CONSUMER *Go to the library or buy a consumer magazine, such as Consumer Report or Consumers Digest. Look up a product that you use or would like to buy. Which brand name(s) does the consumer magazine recommend? What reasons does it give? Does the magazine give the price of the product? Report to your class or to your group on the product that you researched.*

■ C. ADVERTISEMENTS AND COMMERCIALS
Listen to several TV and radio commercials and look at advertisements in magazines. Make a list of three products. What adjectives does each company use to describe its product? What kind of pictures (and music) does the advertisement use? What age group is the company trying to appeal to? Does the advertisement make you want to try this product? Why or why not?

Grammar Summary

■ I. Superlative adjectives

Use the superlative form of the adjective to compare three or more people, places, or things.

The subcompact is **the cheapest** of the three cars.

A sports utility vehicle is **the most expensive** of the three cars.

Adjective		Form
1. One-syllable adjectives		Add **the + est**
fast	→	the fastest
safe		the safest
cheap		the cheapest
2. Two-syllable adjectives that end with y		**the** + change the **y** to **i** and add **est**
early	→	the earliest
heavy		the heaviest
3. Adjectives with two or more syllables		Use **the most** + the adjective
expensive	→	the most expensive
popular		the most popular

2. Irregulars

good	better than	the best
bad	worse than	the worst
far	farther than	the farthest
	more than	the most
	less	the least

13 The Presidents

Past Tense of *Be*

A. THE PRESIDENTS *Can you identify these six presidents? Were they Democrats or Republicans? What do you know about them? Are they all still alive?*

Ronald Reagan	Richard Nixon	George Bush
John F. Kennedy	Lyndon Johnson	Jimmy Carter

> **Past Tense of *Be***
> Carter **was** a Democrat.
> Reagan and Bush **were** Republicans.

B. LISTEN: THE PRESIDENTS—1961 TO PRESENT

*Listen and write the years of each president's term. (A president is elected for a four-year term.) Under **Party**, write **D** for Democrat or **R** for Republican.*

President		Years in Office	Party
35th	John F. Kennedy	1961–	D
36th	Lyndon Johnson		
37th	Richard Nixon		
38th	Gerald Ford		
39th	Jimmy Carter		
40th	Ronald Reagan		
41st	George Bush		
42nd	Bill Clinton		
43rd			
44th			

Complete the chart with any current information.

■ C. ANSWER *Answer these questions about the chart.*

EXAMPLE

Was he a Republican?

Yes, he was.

No, he wasn't.

Were they Democrats?

Yes, they were.

No, they weren't.

1. Was John F. Kennedy a Republican?
2. Was he president from 1961 to 1963?
3. Was he in office one full term? Do you know the reason?
4. Was Lyndon Johnson president after Kennedy?
5. Were Kennedy and Johnson Democrats?
6. Was Nixon a Republican?
7. Was he president for eight full years? Why not?
8. Were Ford and Carter from the same party?
9. Was Reagan president for two terms?
10. Was Bush president for two terms?
11. Were Reagan and Bush both Republicans?
12. Who is the current president?

◼ D. *WHO* QUESTIONS Ask and answer questions about the presidents chart.

1. Who was the president from _____ to _____ ?

2. Who was the president before _____ ?

3. Who was the president after _____ ?

4. Who was the _____ th president?

Working Together

◼ A. WORLD POLITICS Match the political figure and the information on the right.

1. Margaret Thatcher   _____ a. He was the dictator of Haiti from 1971 to 1986.

2. Nelson Mandela   _____ b. He was the president of the Soviet Union during the

transition to an open economy.

3. Lech Walesa   _____ c. He was the first black president of South Africa.

4. Mikhail Gorbachev   _____ d. She was the first female prime minister of Great Britain.

5. Mao Tse-tung   _____ e. He was a labor leader and the president of Poland from

1990 to 1995.

6. Jean Claude Duvalier   _____ f. He was the leader of the Communist Chinese party

from 1931 to 1976.

◼ B. WORLD LEADERS In a group, write the names of seven world leaders or politicians from the present (or the past) on seven index cards. On seven more index cards, write one sentence about each person. Exchange cards with another group. Try to match the person with the information.

◼ C. INTERVIEW Speak with a student from a different country and find out about that country's government. Find the location of the country on a world map. Complete the chart with your information.

1. What country are you from?	
2. What kind of government do you have in your country?	
3. Who is the president of your country?	
4. Was he/she elected?	
5. How often are elections held?	
6. Who was the previous leader of your country?	
7. What is the voting age in your country?	
8. Did you vote in the last election?	

Practicing on Your Own

◼ A. PRESIDENTIAL FACTS *Complete these sentences with **was** or **were**.*

1. George Washington __was__ the first president of the United States.

2. Woodrow Wilson _____ the president during World War I.

3. Franklin Delano Roosevelt and Harry S. Truman _____ the presidents during World War II.

4. John F. Kennedy _____ the youngest person elected as president.

5. Ronald Reagan _____ the oldest president. He _____ 78 when he left office.

6. John Adams _____ the second president of the United States. His son, John Quincy Adams, _____ the sixth president.

7. Many presidents _____ lawyers before they became president.

8. Many recent presidents _____ governors before they became president.

9. Johnson, Nixon, and Ford _____ vice presidents before they became president.

10. Franklin Delano Roosevelt _____ the only president to serve more than two terms as president.

President and Party	Years	Born	Early Career
Jimmy Carter (D)	1977–80	1924–Georgia	peanut farmer, senator, governor of Georgia
Ronald Reagan (R)	1981–89	1911–Illinois	actor, governor of California
George Bush (R)	1989–92	1924–Massachusetts	navy pilot, ambassador to United Nations, vice president, director of CIA
Bill Clinton (D)	1993–	1946–Arkansas	lawyer, governor of Arkansas

1. Were Carter and Clinton both Democrats?   Yes, they were. _____

2. Was Carter a soybean farmer? _____

3. Were all of these presidents governors? _____

4. Was Ronald Reagan a movie actor? _____

5. What year were Carter and Bush born? _____

6. Was George Bush in the army? _____

7. Where was Reagan born? _____

8. Was Reagan the governor of California? _____

9. Was Bush the governor of Massachusetts? _____

10. Was Bush a pilot in the navy? _____

C. RONALD REAGAN   *Read this passage about Ronald Reagan.*

Ronald Reagan was born February 6, 1911, in Tampico, Illinois. His father was a shoe salesperson, and his mother was a housewife. Reagan graduated from Eureka College in 1932, and then he went to Hollywood. He was a sports announcer and an actor during the next 20 years. In 1952, he married Nancy Davis.

Reagan became interested in politics in the 1960s. At first, he was a Democrat. He changed parties in 1962 and became a Republican. He ran for governor of California in 1966 and won. He was in favor of lower taxes and smaller government. He learned from his acting career and was an excellent speaker.

Reagan ran for president and won in 1980. At 70, he was the oldest person ever elected president. Reagan was popular in the United States. He was a conservative and wanted to reduce the size of government. He was able to pass legislation that lowered taxes. This was supposed to balance the national budget. Instead, the national debt increased. Reagan was in favor of a strong defense and supported military spending.

Form questions about the information.

1. Where was Reagan born _____? In Illinois.

2. _____? A shoe salesperson.

3. _____? For twenty years.

4. _____? A Democrat.

5. _____? Lower taxes.

6. _____? Yes, he was.

7. _____? 70 years old.

8. _____? A strong defense.

Sharing Our Stories

A FAMOUS PERSON   *Write about a famous person in the history of your country or in the history of the United States. When was this person born? What was this person's position? What did this person accomplish? Was this person popular? How is he or she remembered today?*

Having Fun with the Language

■ A. HOW GOVERNMENT WORKS *Sit in a small group. How much do you know about the government of the United States? Complete this information.*

population	Congress	two	House of Representatives
president	vice president	nine	Supreme Court
Senate	Constitution	Cabinet	commander-in-chief
president	amendments	1787	

The ___Constitution___ is the document that created the government of the United States. It was written in _____. It established three branches of government: the executive, headed by the _____, the legislative, which is the _____, and the judicial, which is the _____ and other federal courts. The first ten _____ to the Constitution explain the basic rights of all American citizens. Seventeen additional amendments provide other rights and protections.

The president is the head of the executive branch. The president works with the _____ and the _____, which is a group of advisors. The president recommends policies, enforces the laws of the country, and is the _____ of the U.S. armed forces. The Congress passes the laws that govern the country. It consists of the _____ and the _____. The Senate has 100 members, _____ from each state. The House of Representatives has 435 members, and the number of representatives each state has is based on the state's _____. The Supreme Court reviews the laws of the country to be sure they do not violate the Constitution. There are _____ justices on the Supreme Court, and they serve for life. The _____ appoints the justices with the approval of the Senate.

B. HISTORICAL FIGURES *Who was this person? Use an encyclopedia or almanac and find five facts about one of these people in American history.*

Abraham Lincoln   Sacajawea   Martin Luther King, Jr.

Thomas Jefferson   Lewis and Clark   Harriet Tubman

Clara Barton   Robert E. Lee   Susan B. Anthony

Grammar Summary

I. Past statements: *be*

Carter	was	a Democrat.
Kennedy and Johnson	were	Democrats.

2. *Yes/no questions*

Was	I he she	a Democrat?
Were	we you they	Republicans?

Short answers

Yes, you were.	No, you weren't.
Yes, he was.	No, he wasn't.
Yes, she was.	No, she wasn't.
Yes, you were.	No, you weren't.
Yes, we were.	No, we weren't.
Yes, they were.	No, they weren't.

3. Wh questions

When was Johnson in office?	He was in office from 1963 to 1968.
How long was he in office?	He was in office for five years.
Who was president after Kennedy?	Johnson was.

Moving

Past Tense

Regular Verbs

A. LISTEN: THE MOVE *Miguel and Ana just moved into a new apartment. Listen to the story and number the pictures from 1 to 6.*

B. PAST TENSE *Write the past time of these regular verbs.*
Refer to pages 59 and 145 for spelling rules.

help _helped_   wax _____

fix _____   change _____

borrow _____   move _____

wash _____   carry _____

order _____   paint _____

Complete these sentences about Miguel and Ana's move with a past tense verb from the list above.

1. Miguel and Ana _moved_____ into their new apartment on Saturday.

2. Their family and friends _____ them move.

3. Ana _____ the cabinets.

4. Miguel _____ the floors.

5. The landlord _____ the bedroom blue and the living room beige.

6. He _____ the locks on the doors.

7. The landlord _____ a leaky pipe.

8. Miguel _____ a van from a friend.

9. Their friends _____ boxes and furniture all day.

10. In the evening, Miguel _____ pizza for everyone.

C. LISTEN: PRONUNCIATION *Listen to these past tense verbs. Write the number of syllables you hear in each verb. Repeat the verbs.*

1. changed _1___   5. painted _____   9. carried _____

2. rented _____   6. helped _____   10. wanted _____

3. looked _____   7. called _____   11. lived _____

4. needed _____   8. started _____   12. fixed _____

Look at the pictures and retell the story using the verbs above.

◼ D. MOVING
When did you move into your current house or apartment? Check all the sentences that describe your move and read them to a partner. Add two more sentences.

_____ 1. I packed all my things.

_____ 2. I painted one or more of the rooms.

_____ 3. I filled out a change-of-address form at the post office.

_____ 4. I called the phone company.

_____ 5. I waited for the phone company to install a new phone line.

_____ 6. I cleaned the apartment/house.

_____ 7. I rented a truck.

_____ 8. I borrowed a van.

_____ 9. I signed a lease.

_____ 10. My friends and family helped me.

_____ 11. _____.

_____ 12. _____.

Irregular Verbs

◼ A. IRREGULAR PAST VERBS
Write these irregular verbs in the past tense. Refer to the Irregular Verb Chart in the appendix.

speak _spoke_ _____

ring _____

tell _____

break _____

get _____

put _____

be _____

drive _____

pay _____

see _____

steal _____

B. LISTEN: FINDING AN APARTMENT *Put your pencil down and listen twice to Miguel and Ana's story about finding their new apartment. Then try to complete the story with the verbs from Exercise A.*

We __were_____ lucky in finding our current apartment. Before this, we lived in a

different town, but we _____ happy there. The area _____ safe,

and last month someone _____ into our apartment and _____

our TV and stereo. We talked to friends and looked in the paper, but we didn't find anything.

Then one day we _____ in the car and _____ around in a neighbor-

hood we both liked. We _____ on a quiet street a few blocks from town when

we _____ a two-family house with a sign in the window, "Apartment for Rent,

Inquire Within." We _____ the doorbell. The owner _____ home,

and he showed us around the apartment. It _____ sunny and clean with lots

of room. We signed a lease that day and _____ him one month's rent and a

security deposit. We were very lucky! The owner _____ us, "I just

_____ the sign in the window this morning!"

■ C. HOW DID YOU FIND YOUR APARTMENT? *Check the sentence that describes how you found your current house or apartment.*

_____ A friend told me about the apartment.

_____ I read an ad in the newspaper.

_____ I saw a sign on a building.

_____ I went to a real estate agency.

_____ _____

Negatives

◼ A. MEMORIES *Think of your home before you came to this country. Circle the information that is true for you.*

1. I   **lived   didn't live**   in the city.

2. I   **lived   didn't live**   in the country.

3. I   **lived   didn't live**   in a house.

4. I   **lived   didn't live**   in an apartment.

5. We   **moved   didn't move**   when I lived in my country.

6. I   **walked   didn't walk**   to school.

7. I   **had   didn't have**   my own bedroom.

8. My family   **had   didn't have**   a garden.

9. We   **grew   didn't grow**   our own vegetables.

10. We   **knew   didn't know**   our neighbors.

11. We   **felt   didn't feel**   safe.

12. We   **had   didn't have**   a patio.

What other memories do you have of your home in your native country?

◼ B. LET'S MOVE! *Miguel and Ana didn't like their last apartment. They had many reasons to move. Compare their new apartment and their last apartment.*

EXAMPLE

They have a parking space.   →   They didn't have a parking space.

Their landlord fixes problems.   →   Their landlord didn't fix problems.

The area is safe.   →   The area wasn't safe.

1. The bus stops near their apartment.

2. The neighbors speak with them.

3. They like the landlord.

4. The landlord shovels the sidewalk after it snows.

5. The apartment has lots of closets.

6. The apartment is sunny.

7. The landlord allows them to have a pet.

8. The apartment has two bedrooms.

9. The area is quiet.

10. The landlord changed the locks.

Compare your current home with your last home. Name three differences.

Questions

■ A. APARTMENT PROBLEMS *Ask your partner these questions and check his or her answer. If your partner answered* **Yes** *to any questions, ask for more information.*

Past Tense—*Yes/No Questions*
Did he **pay** the rent?
Did you **move** last year?

EXAMPLE

Student A: I lost the key to my apartment.

Student B: What did you do? Did you call the landlord?

Student A: Yes, but I had to wait all afternoon for him to come home.

1. Did you ever lose your apartment key?	❏ Yes, I did.	❏ No, I didn't.
2. Did the heat ever go off?	❏ Yes, it did.	❏ No, it didn't.
3. Did you ever pay your rent late?	❏ Yes, I did.	❏ No, I didn't.
4. Did you ever break a window?	❏ Yes, I did.	❏ No, I didn't.
5. Did the electricity ever go off?	❏ Yes, it did.	❏ No, it didn't.
6. Did you ever have a problem with the toilet?	❏ Yes, I did.	❏ No, I didn't.
7. Did you ever ask the landlord to paint your apartment?	❏ Yes, I did.	❏ No, I didn't.

B. GARAGE SALES

Use your imagination and complete the missing information in this paragraph. Then answer the questions about the story.

Miguel and Ana needed more furniture and household items for their apartment. The weekend after they moved in, they went to several garage sales.* At the first one, they saw a _____ they liked. The price was $ _____ . Miguel offered the owner $ _____ ; they agreed on $ _____ . At another garage sale, they found a _____ for the kitchen that Ana loved. They paid $ _____ for it. At their last stop, they saw a _____ . Ana said they didn't need it, but Miguel loved it! They bought it for $ _____ .

*Garage sales are sometimes called yard sales or tag sales. Do you have them in your country?

1. Where did Miguel and Ana look for furniture and household items?
2. What did they see at the first garage sale?
3. What was the price?
4. How much did Miguel offer the owner?
5. What price did they agree on?
6. What did they find for the kitchen?
7. How much did they pay for it?
8. What did they see at their last stop?
9. Did Ana think that they should buy it? Did they buy it?
10. How much did they pay for it?

> **Past Tense—Questions**
> When **did** she **move**?
> When **did** you **move**?
> Where **did** they **move**?

C. LISTEN: CHIN-HAO'S STORY

Chin-Hao is a young man from China. Listen to his story and take notes.

1992	23 years old, uncle, shoe factory
1993	
1994	
1996	
1997	

Use the cues. Ask and answer questions about Chin-Hao's life.

Cue: When/come/U.S.? → When did Chin-Hao come to the U.S.?   He came in 1992.

Cue: How old/be/he? → How old was he?   He was 23.

1. he / speak English?
2. Who / he / live with?
3. Where / he / find a job?
4. Where / he / move / in 1993?
5. When / he / study English?
6. When / he / find / a better job?

7. Why / he / move?
8. When / Chin-Hao / begin college?
9. What / he / decide to study?
10. Who / he / meet?
11. When / they / get married?
12. What / they / do now?

◼ D. WHY MOVE? *Americans move approximately 11 times in a lifetime. The graph shows the most common reasons.*

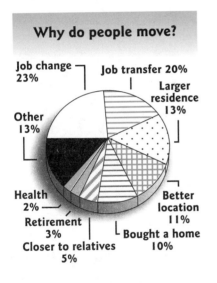

Why do people move?

Job change 23%
Job transfer 20%
Larger residence 13%
Other 13%
Health 2%
Retirement 3%
Closer to relatives 5%
Bought a home 10%
Better location 11%

1. What is the most common reason that people move?

2. What percentage of people move from an apartment to a house?

3. What percentage of people are moving to be closer to their families?

4. What was the reason for your last move?

5. How often do people in your country move? What do you think is the most common reason?

A. INTERVIEW *Interview a partner about his or her first year in the United States.*

The past of **can** is **could**.

1. What country are you from?		
2. When did you come to the United States?		
3. Where did you live at first?		
4. Who did you live with?		
5. Who helped you when you first came here?		
6. Could you speak English?	Yes	No
7. Did you have any friends here?	Yes	No
8. Did you like the food?	Yes	No
9. Did you like the weather?	Yes	No
10. Could you drive?	Yes	No
11. Did you have a car?	Yes	No
12. Could you find a job?	Yes	No
13. Were you homesick?	Yes	No

B. DISCUSSION *In a group, talk about your first year in this country. Again, tell your group the country you are from and the year you came to the United States.*

1. Why did you decide to come to the United States?
2. Did you have family or friends here?
3. What did you expect to find in the United States? A job? A house? Education?
4. What was your biggest problem in your first week? In your first year?
5. What did you do about this problem?
6. What else was difficult for you?
7. Do you feel different now from when you first came here?

■ C. THEN AND NOW

How is your life now different from life in your native country? Compare the two. Use these phrases to help you, but think of others that contrast your life then and now.

watch TV	eat _____ food	cook outside
wear _____	go to the market every day	eat at fast-food restaurants
have a computer	work	know my neighbors

Then	Now
I didn't eat at fast-food restaurants.	I eat at a fast-food restaurant about once a week.
I didn't have a computer.	We have a computer at home.

D. STUDENT TO STUDENT *Match the questions and answers.*

Student A: *Ask **Student B** questions 1 to 4 below. Listen carefully and write the answers.*
Student B: *Turn to page 186.*

1. When did David and Lynn move?

   _____

2. Where did they move?

   _____

3. Why did they move?

   _____

4. Did they move to a bigger place?

   _____

When you finish, change pages. **Student B** *will ask questions 5 to 8 below and write the answers.* **Student A** *will turn to page 186 and answer the questions.*

5. Did they rent a truck?

   _____

6. Where did they live before this?

   _____

7. How did they find the apartment?

   _____

8. What did they like about it?

   _____

Practicing On Your Own

■ A. MY FIRST APARTMENT *Mia is writing about her first apartment. Complete these sentences with the correct form of the past tense verb.*

1. Mia ___*didn't like*_____ (like—negative) her first apartment.

2. She _____ (live) on the fourth floor.

3. She _____ (have—negative) an elevator. She

   _____ (have) to carry everything up four floors.

4. One day the hall light _____ (go) out. She

   _____ (call) the landlord several times.

5. He _____ (return—negative) any of her phone calls.

6. The neighbors on her left _____ (play) loud music.

7. The neighbors on her right _____ (have) a baby. He

   _____ (cry) all night.

8. The neighbors upstairs _____ (fight) all the time.

9. The air conditioner _____ (work—negative).

10. Mia _____ (can sleep—negative) at night.

■ B. MY CHILDHOOD HOME *Answer these questions about your childhood home.*

1. Did you live in the city? _____

2. Did you live in the country? _____

3. Did your family own a house or an apartment? _____

4. Was your home large? _____

5. Did your grandparents live with you? _____

6. Did you have a yard? _____

7. Did you have a garden? What kind? _____

8. Did you raise any animals? _____

9. Did you live near town? _____

10. Were your neighbors friendly? _____

11. Was your neighborhood safe? _____

12. Did you lock your doors at night? _____

■ C. TENSE CONTRAST *Write the verbs in the correct tense: present, present continuous, past, and future.*

Last year, Boris and Nadia __decided__ (decide) to move to a new apartment. They _____ (like) the old neighborhood, but their apartment _____ (be) too small. They _____ (need) more bedrooms. They _____ (look) for about a month and _____ (find) an apartment in a small building near town. They only _____ (see) the neighborhood in the daytime, never at night.

Boris and Nadia and their family _____ now _____ (live) in the new apartment. They _____ (move) in four months ago. This time, they _____ (love) the apartment. It's on the first floor, and it _____ (have) three bedrooms and two bathrooms. The landlord always _____ (fix) anything that's broken. Last month, Boris _____ (be) two days late with the rent, but the landlord _____ (say— negative) anything.

But Boris and Nadia _____ (hate) the neighborhood. In the daytime, it's quiet. At night, it's a different story. Teenagers and young men _____ (stand) on the street corner and _____ (talk) loudly. Cars _____ (drive) up and down the street playing their car stereos very loud. Also, Nadia _____ (feel—negative) safe on the street. Last week, someone _____ (break) into their car and _____ (steal) the radio. Nadia _____ (want) to move, and Boris _____ (feel) the same. Next week, they _____ (look) for another apartment. This time, they _____ (check) it out in the day and in the evening.

Write the question for each answer.

1. __Did they like the old neighborhood_____? Yes, they did.
2. _____? It was too small.
3. _____? In the daytime.
4. _____? Three.
5. _____? Yes, he does.
6. _____? The neighborhood.
7. _____? At night.
8. _____? No, she doesn't.
9. _____? The radio.
10. _____? Next week.

Read Tami's story about her move from Rhode Island to California.

I am an English-as-a-foreign-language teacher and last summer I moved from Rhode Island back to California. I like the sunny skies and warm weather there better than the cold winters of the Northeast, so I spent all summer looking for a job in California. I finally found a new job for the fall in San Diego. Two weeks before I moved, I went to the post office and filled out a change-of-address form. Then I spent time looking for empty boxes at local stores and I reserved a rental van. After my summer job was over, I began packing. I put all my books, files, dishes, and other things in the boxes and my clothes in suitcases. I don't have a lot of things, so it only took me about three hours to pack the van and clean the apartment. I wanted to make sure the apartment was in good condition when I left. After the landlord inspected the apartment, she gave me my security deposit. Then I began the drive to California. To break up the trip, I stopped to visit friends along the way. It took me about ten days to drive to San Diego.

Tami Nassiri

Write about your move to this country or from one location to another. Why did you move? What preparations did you make for the move? What did you pack? How did you move your furniture, your clothes, and your other things.

■ **A. THE THINGS I LEFT BEHIND** *What are two items that you left in your native country that you didn't bring here or that you couldn't bring here? Tell your group about each one and why you miss it.*

> **EXAMPLE**
>
> I miss my garden. I had a small vegetable garden where I raised tomatoes and peppers and other vegetables. I grew delicious tomatoes and gave them to my friends and neighbors. Here, I live in an apartment and can't have a garden.

■ **B. ROLE PLAY** *Write and act out a conversation between a landlord and a prospective tenant. Ask about the rent, security deposit, the utilities, pets, public transportation, parking, and the length of the lease.*

Grammar Summary

■ **1. Past tense**

In the simple past tense, we talk about things we did in the past (yesterday, last week, etc.).

Regular past verbs end with **ed.**

The chart of irregular past verbs is on page 181 in the appendix.

■ **2. Statements**

I We You They He She It	liked painted rented	the apartment.

■ **3. Negatives**

I We You They He She It	didn't didn't did not	like paint rent	the apartment.

4. *Yes/no questions*

	Short answers	
Did I **pay** the rent ?	Yes, you did.	No, you didn't.
Did you **sign** a lease?	Yes, I did.	No, I didn't.
Did he **move** yesterday?	Yes, he did.	No, he didn't.
Did she **buy** a sofa?	Yes, she did.	No, she didn't.
Did it **start?**	Yes, it did.	No, it didn't.
Did we **change** the locks?	Yes, we did.	No, we didn't.
Did you **buy** a table?	Yes, we did.	No, we didn't.
Did they **paint** the kitchen?	Yes, they did.	No, they didn't.

5. *Wh* questions

When **did** he **move?**	He moved last year.
Why **did** he **move?**	His rent was too high.
Where **did** he **find** an apartment?	He found one on Broad Street.

6. *Who* questions (subject)

Who **helped** you move?	My brother **did.**
Who **fixed** the light?	The landlord **did.**

7. Spelling

Verb ending		Spelling
1. Most verbs		Add **ed.**
open	→	open**ed**
mail		mail**ed**
walk		walk**ed**
2. Verbs that end with **e**		Add **d.**
smile	→	smil**ed**
arrive		arriv**ed**
3. Verbs that end with a consonant, vowel, consonant		Double the final consonant.
stop	→	stop**ped**
rob		rob**bed**
Do not double a final **w, x,** or **y.**		
fix		fix**ed**
play		play**ed**
4. Verbs that end with a consonant and **y**		Change the **y** to **i,** and add **ed.**
try	→	tri**ed**
study		stud**ied**

15 The Great Outdoors

Infinitives

■ **A. CAMPING EQUIPMENT** *Repeat the name of each camping item after your teacher. Ask about any new words.*

backpack ____   sun block ____   tent ____   fishing rod ____   fresh water ____

sleeping bag ____   matches ____   flashlight ____   compass ____   insect repellent ____

first-aid kit ____   camping stove ____   cooler ____   camera ____

Write the correct vocabulary word on each item in the picture.

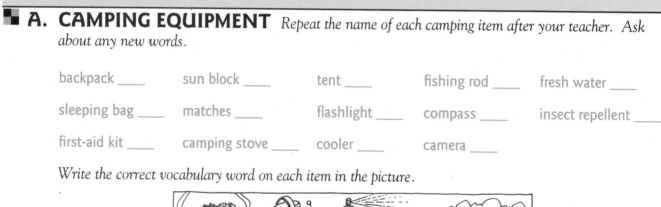

What other items do you need to take on a camping trip?

146

■■■

B. LISTEN: GETTING READY *Andre and Marie are planning to go camping this weekend. Listen to their conversation. Check the items that they already have. Circle the items that they need to buy or find.*

tent ✓   fishing rod   insect repellent

sleeping bags   matches   sun block

stove   camera   first-aid kit

cooler   film   flashlight

backpacks   compass

> **Infinitives**
> Many verbs are followed by the infinitive form.
> They need **to bring** a tent.
> He has **to buy** some film.

■ C. NEED TO, HAVE TO *Read each sentence about the camping trip and decide what Andre and Marie* **have to** *or* **need to** *bring.*

EXAMPLE

There aren't any cabins or motels at the campsite.

They have to bring a tent.   *or*

They need to bring a tent.

1. There aren't any beds at the campsite.

2. Andre hopes to catch some fish.

3. When they are hiking, they don't want to get lost.

4. They can't drink the lake water.

5. There are a lot of mosquitoes and other insects outdoors, especially at night.

6. Andre wants to have a small fire every night.

7. Marie wants to take pictures of the wildlife and the flowers.

8. Marie sometimes gets a bad sunburn.

9. There aren't any refrigerators at the campsite.

10. At night, there are no lights.

D. PLAN TO, HOPE TO

We can make specific plans about events that we can control:
Andre and Marie **plan to bring** a fishing rod.

We can hope something will happen, but we don't have control over it:
Andre and Marie **hope to catch** a lot of fish.

Use the phrases below. What do Andre and Marie plan to do? What do they hope will happen? In some cases, both words are correct.

climb a mountain	**bring a fishing rod**	**take a camera and film**
see some wildlife	**have sunny weather**	**find a beautiful campsite**
catch a lot of fish	**have a wonderful time**	**cook on a camp stove**

What do you plan to do this summer? What do you hope will happen this summer?

Working Together

A. INTERVIEW
Ask your partner about these outdoor activities. Check the 😊 *if your partner likes the activity. Check the* 😞 *if your partner doesn't like the activity.*

EXAMPLE

hike   Do you like to hike?   Yes, I do.

                                      No, I don't.

hike	😊	😞	drive in the country	😊	😞
sail	😊	😞	garden	😊	😞
play tennis	😊	😞	walk in the park	😊	😞
jog	😊	😞	canoe	😊	😞
cook outside	😊	😞	fish	😊	😞
bike	😊	😞	lie in the sun	😊	😞
swim	😊	😞	sit and watch the world go by	😊	😞
roller blade	😊	😞	surf	😊	😞

Compare your charts and complete the sentences.

1. We both like to _____ .

2. My partner likes to _____ , and I do, too.

3. I like to _____ , and my partner does, too.

4. I don't like to _____ , and my partner doesn't, either.

5. My partner likes to _____ , but I don't.

6. I like to _____ , but my partner doesn't.

■ B. GETTING THE CAR READY

*Your family is planning to drive to your sister's house next week, about 1,000 miles from home. You need to get the car ready for the trip. Read each statement and talk about what you **need to do** or **have to do**.*

> **EXAMPLE**
>
> The right front blinker doesn't work.　→　I have to fix the blinker.

1. Your last oil change was 5,000 miles ago.
2. The front tires look a little low.
3. The car is dirty, both inside and out.
4. There's no window washing fluid in the washer fluid tank.
5. You aren't sure of the best way to get there.
6. You have a first aid kit; you think it's in the bathroom.
7. The trunk is filled with four months of junk.
8. You're not sure where you put the car registration.
9. The spare tire looked good about a year ago, but you haven't looked at it since.

■ C. A GROUP OUTING

As a group, choose a place to visit for the day. It should be within a hundred miles of your school. Make plans based on the questions below.

1. Where are you going to go?
2. How are you going to get there?
3. What do you need to bring?
4. Is there an entrance fee? How much do you have to pay?
5. How much money do you each plan to bring?
6. Do you have to bring a lunch (or picnic), or do you plan to buy lunch?
7. What do you plan to do there?
8. What kind of weather do you hope to have?
9. What day do you plan to go?
10. What time do you plan to leave? What time do you expect to return?

D. STUDENT TO STUDENT: THE FISHING TRIP

Student A: *You and your partner are packing for a fishing trip tomorrow. Ask about each of the following items, using the questions below as examples. Check the items you have. Circle the items that you need to find, pack, or buy.*

Student B: *Turn to page 186.*

EXAMPLE

A: **Did you pack** the fishing rods?   B: Yes, I did.   *or*   No, I didn't.

A: **Did you remember** to bring the hooks?   B: No, I have to find them.

A: **How about** the worms?   B: We need to buy them in the morning.

the fishing rods   the hat   the net

the hooks   the sun block   the cooler

the worms   the insect repellent   the fishing license

Practicing on Your Own

◼ A. COMPLETE *Choose the correct verb and complete each sentence with an infinitive.*

see	camp	catch	keep	have
lie	bring	wear	take	

1. Andre and Marie plan ___to camp___ by a small lake.

2. Marie plans _____ a lot of pictures with her camera.

3. They have _____ fresh water with them.

4. They need _____ their food in a cooler.

5. Andre hopes _____ some fish.

6. Marie wants _____ in the sun and read.

7. They need _____ a stove, a pot, and food with them.

8. At night, they need _____ warm clothing.

9. They hope to _____ beautiful weather.

10. Marie hopes _____ some deer.

■ B. THE CAMPING TRIP *Write a statement about each of these situations. Use one of these infinitives in each sentence.*

need to   have to   hope to

want to   plan to   would like to

1. You're going to take a long drive. The gas tank is almost empty.

   We have to stop for gas.

2. You're not sure how to get to the national park.

   _____

3. Everyone over 14 has to have a fishing license.

   _____

4. You forgot to make a reservation for a campsite.

   _____

5. The sun is hot, and the water looks inviting.

   _____

6. You've been standing in the water for two hours, and you still haven't caught a fish.

   _____

7. It's starting to rain.

   _____

■ C. THE GRAND CANYON *Read about a popular vacation in Grand Canyon National Park.*

The Grand Canyon is located in northwest Arizona. This spectacular canyon is a deep gorge cut into the earth by the Colorado River millions of years ago. The canyon winds for almost 220 miles, ranges 4 to 14 miles wide, and is up to one mile deep.

Over 4 million tourists visit Grand Canyon National Park every year. Raft trips down the Colorado River are a popular way of experiencing the canyon. Small and large raft groups ride down the Colorado River, led by experienced tour guides. The ride is peaceful and quiet as the rafts glide through the breathtaking scenery, with ongoing lectures on the history of the canyon, rock formations, the wildlife and river. The guides warn of the approach to the rapids. As the rafts pass through stronger rapids of grade 4, 5, and higher, passengers hang onto ropes on the inside of the rafts and enjoy the thrill of the ride . Everyone wears life vests at all times and passengers have to learn what to do if the raft capsizes or if they are thrown overboard. In the afternoon, the guides find a camping site by the side of the river and the rafters set up their tents while the guides set up the kitchen. There are hikes to side canyons, ridges, and waterfalls. Evening dinner is prepared by the guides and after dinner, people sit around the fire and talk about the adventures of their day.

Use these cues to write questions and answers about rafting through the Grand Canyon. The answers are in parentheses. Use a separate sheet of paper.

1. When / I / need / make / a reservation / for a raft trip? (6 months before the trip)

   When do I need to make a reservation for a raft trip?

   You need to make a reservation 6 months before the trip.

2. When / many people / plan / take / raft trips? (in the spring)

3. What / passengers / need / wear / at all times? (life jacket)

4. What / passengers / have / learn? (what to do if the boat capsizes)

5. When / you / hope / visit / the Grand Canyon?

Sharing Our Stories

Write about a national park, state park, or other recreation area that you have visited. Where is it? Describe it. What can you do there? Do you have to pay an admission fee? What do you need to bring? When did you go there? Write about your experience.

Having Fun with the Language

A. CAMPING ESSENTIALS *These are some popular items that campers take on a hike or a camping trip. Describe each item. Why is it important?*

stake	lantern	compass
whistle	binoculars	water filter
altimeter		

B. CAMPING EMERGENCIES *What do you **need to do** or **have to do** in each emergency?*

1. You get lost on a high mountain in the deep woods.
2. You see a bear.
3. You are on a boat in the middle of a lake. You are rowing your boat, and you drop an oar.
4. A snake bites you.
5. You and a friend are hiking in the woods, and you break your ankle.

Grammar Summary

I. Infinitives

Many common verbs are followed by an infinitive (*to* + the simple form of a verb):

want	need	have
like	hate	plan
hope	decide	would like

I plan **to go** camping.

We hope **to have** a great time.

She needs **to bring** food.

Working Parents

Present Time Clauses

 A. LISTEN: A WORKING MOTHER *Look at the picture and listen to this story about a working mother and her family.*

Repeat these verbs from the story after your teacher. Ask about any new words.

get up—gets up
kiss—kisses
get dressed—gets dressed
drop off—drops off
buckle—buckles

jump out of—jumps out of
wake up—wakes up
climb—climbs
put on—puts on

Present Time Clause	
Main clause	**Time** clause
Bob takes a shower	after he gets up.
He eats breakfast	before he goes to work.

■ **B. TALKING ABOUT THE STORY** *Answer these questions about the story.*

1. Who gets up first?
2. When does Pat get up?
3. What does Bob do after he takes a shower?
4. What does Pat do after she wakes up?
5. What does Bob do before he leaves for work?
6. When does Pat eat breakfast with the boys?
7. When does Pat get dressed?
8. What does Pat do before she starts the car?
9. Where does Pat bring the kids before she goes to work?
10. Why aren't Pat's customers angry when she's late?

■ **C. TIME WORDS** *Complete these sentences with **before, after, when,** or **as soon as.** For some sentences, more than one answer is possible.*

1. _As soon as_____ the alarm rings, Bob gets up.

2. Bob takes a shower _____ Pat gets up.

3. _____ Bob gets out of the shower, he wakes Pat up.

4. _____ the boys wake up, they watch a video.

5. _____ Bob eats breakfast, Timmy watches a video.

6. Bob kisses everyone good-bye _____ he leaves for work.

7. David and Timmy eat breakfast _____ their mother eats.

8. _____ everyone is ready, they leave.

9. The kids always get in their car seats _____ they get in the car.

10. Pat's customers don't get angry _____ she's late.

155

D. MY DAY *Sit with a small group and answer these questions about your day.*

1. What do you do when you get up?
2. Are you the first one in your family to get up in the morning?
3. Do you do exercises after you get up?
4. Do you eat breakfast before you leave your home?
5. What do you do before you go to school?
6. Who do you talk to before class begins?
7. What do you do as soon as class is over?
8. What do you like to do when you get home?
9. What do you usually do after dinner is finished?
10. What do you do before you go to bed?

Working Together

A. MY TEACHER'S SCHEDULE *Listen to your teacher talk about his or her schedule. As you listen, write in the time that your teacher gets up, works, exercises, etc., and complete the chart below. Then ask your teacher about his or her schedule.*

EXAMPLE

What do you do as soon as you get to school?

When do you eat lunch?

Do you correct our papers before you leave school or after you get home?

Time	Activity
	get up

◼ B. BEFORE OR AFTER *Work with a partner or a small group. Read the two actions in the box. Explain the order in which you usually do the two actions.*

I put on my seat belt before I start the car.   *or*

I put on my seat belt after I start the car.

put on my seat belt start the car	return my library books my library books are due
turn out the light get into bed	make a dental appointment have a dental problem
do my homework eat dinner	return to my car the parking meter time expires
get paid pay my bills	stop talking the teacher enters the room

C. STUDENT TO STUDENT

Student A: Your partner will read five sentences about working parents, but only three are true. Write the three sentences that you think are true. Check your answers on page 161.
Student B: Turn to page 187.

1. _____
   _____

2. _____
   _____

3. _____
   _____

When you finish, change pages. **Student A** *will read five new sentences, and* **Student B** *will write the three that he or she thinks are true.*

◼ A. STRESSFUL SITUATIONS *Complete these sentences about yourself. How do you handle stress in your busy life? Compare your answers with a partner's.*

1. When I can't get to sleep, I _____.

2. When I need to relax, I _____.

3. When I work too hard, I _____.

4. When I'm tired, I _____.

5. When I'm stuck in traffic, I _____.

6. When I'm late for an appointment, I _____.

7. When I don't feel like going to school, I _____.

8. When I have a test, I _____.

◼ B. STORY *Read this story about a busy family.*

Mr. and Mrs. Butler have three children, a daughter, Jessica, who is in eighth grade, and five-year-old twins, David and Joanna. Last year, after 20 years at a telecommunications company, Mr. Butler lost his job. The company downsized, and 1,000 employees were let go. When he lost his job, Mrs. Butler had to go back to work. She's a computer programmer, and now she goes to work five days a week. When there's an important project, she works late at night and even weekends. Mr. Butler stays home and takes care of the children and the house. He's a homemaker now.

When Mrs. Butler leaves for work, she drops the children off at their schools. Then she drives to work downtown. When she gets to work, she usually gets a cup of coffee and talks with her co-workers. Then, she checks her e-mail and answers her messages. After she answers all her messages, she works on her current project. When she has a problem, she consults her project supervisor. If she's very busy, she skips lunch or orders out. When everything goes well, she leaves at 6:00, but if there's a problem, she stays late.

At the same time, Mr. Butler takes care of the home. He's getting used to staying home and taking care of the house.

Answer these questions about the story in a complete sentence.

1. How many children do the Butlers have?

    They have three children.

2. When did Mr. Butler lose his job?

    _____

3. What does Mrs. Butler do when there's an important project?

_____

4. What does Mr. Butler do when his wife is at work?

_____

5. When does Mrs. Butler have a cup of coffee?

_____

6. What does Mrs. Butler do before she works on her current project?

_____

7. If Mrs. Butler is very busy, does she eat lunch?

_____

8. What time does Mrs. Butler leave work?

_____

■ C. MR. BUTLER'S DAY *Combine each pair of sentences into one longer sentence with the time word in parentheses. Change repeated subjects to pronouns.*

EXAMPLE

Mr. Butler finishes the dishes. Mr. Butler does the laundry. (after)

After Mr. Butler finishes the dishes, he does the laundry.

1. Everyone leaves. Mr. Butler does the dishes. (when)
2. The twins come home. Mr. Butler reads the classified ads and sends out résumés. (before)
3. Mr. Butler makes lunch. Mr. Butler picks up the twins. (after)
4. Mr. Butler feeds the twins. Mr. Butler and the twins get back home. (when)
5. The twins play in the yard. Mr. Butler cleans the kitchen. (while)
6. Jessica comes home. Mr. Butler helps Jessica with her homework. (when)
7. Mr. and Mrs. Butler want to go out for an evening. Jessica baby-sits the twins. (when)
8. The family has dinner together. Mrs. Butler gets home at 6:30. (if)

Sharing Our Stories

Nancy and Oscar are working parents with a four-year-old son. Read about a typical day in their family.

Nancy Mulhall-Guillen, husband Oscar Guillen, and their son, Edward, live in an apartment in New Jersey. Nancy is American, and Oscar is from El Salvador. Nancy teaches elementary school, and Oscar is a cook and a part-time caterer. Edward is in preschool.

On a typical weekday, Nancy gets up at 5:45 and gets herself ready for the day. She wakes up Edward at 6:30. Nancy doesn't eat breakfast in the morning; she eats at school. Edward eats wherever he's going that day, at his grandmother's house or at the baby-sitter's house. When Nancy leaves the house, she has so many things to carry that Oscar usually takes all of the things to the car, sometimes even her purse.

Before Nancy goes to work, she drops off Edward at her mother's house or the baby-sitter's. In the past, Edward stayed with both of his grandmothers. He calls them his "English" grandmother and his "Spanish" grandmother. His "Spanish" grandmother is working now, so he sometimes stays with a baby-sitter. From 12:00 to 3:00, Edward goes to school.

When Nancy doesn't have any meetings, she picks up Edward after school. If she has a meeting, he stays wherever he is. It's very convenient. She doesn't have to worry about her son. When Edward is sick, Nancy sometimes has to stay home with him.

In the evening, Oscar cooks. Oscar always cooks. The family eats dinner together when Nancy is home. Nancy also teaches ESL part time two nights a week at the community college. Oscar always has something ready for Nancy's dinner if she's late. After dinner, they watch the Spanish language soap operas every night at 8:00. They usually go to bed at around 11:00. It's a busy day for everyone in the family.

by Nancy Mulhall-Guillen as told to Liz Neblett

Write about your family. How many people live at home? How many children are there, and how old are they? What are the child care arrangements? How do the members of the family share the child care and the household responsibilities? What does each person do to help?

■ A. LIBRARY ASSIGNMENT *Find one of the magazines below in your school or public library. Look in the table of contents and read an article that interests you. Make a copy of the article and bring it to the next class. Tell your classmates about the article.*

Working Mother   Parents   Working Women

■ B. ROLE PLAY: FINDING A NANNY *Get into groups of four students and practice role playing this situation. A mother and father are interviewing two nannies in order to find the perfect nanny to care for their child. One or two groups should volunteer to act out their interviews for the class.*

Two students: You are the parents of a three-year-old child. You both work and need someone to take care of your child. Prepare a list of questions to ask the prospective nannies. Then interview your two applicants, one at a time. After the interviews, select a nanny.

Two students: Both of you are applying to be the nanny of a career couple who need someone to take care of their three-year-old child. Be prepared to answer questions about your background and experience to satisfy your potential employer. You will be interviewed individually.

Grammar Summary

■ 1. Present time clauses

A time clause begins with words such as *before* or *after*. A time clause has a subject and a verb. In present tense time clauses, both the verb in the main clause and verb in the time clause are in the present tense.

Main clause	Time clause
He does the laundry	**after** he cleans the kitchen.

Time clause	Main clause
After he cleans the kitchen,	he does the laundry.

Note: If the time clause is at the beginning of the sentence, use a comma to separate it from the main clause.

Answers for Unit 16

D. Student to Student (page 157)

Working Fathers: 1. True   2. True   3. ~~False~~   4. ~~True~~   5. False (They <u>are</u> happy that their wives work.)

Working Mothers: 1. True   2. False (Only 23% go to day care.)   3. True   4. False (Thirty percent of wives earn as much or more as their husbands.)   5. True

17 The Robbery

Past Time Clauses

Grammar in Action

A. LISTEN: THE ROBBERY

Last night, Spike and Tina tried to rob a jewelry store. Repeat these verbs after your teacher and ask about any new words. Then, look at the pictures and listen to the story.

Past Time Clause	
Main clause	**Time**
Before Spike got out of the car,	he put on black gloves
When the police saw him,	they chased him down the alley.

put on	walk around	climb into	step on	pick up	jump out of
chase	climb over	drive away	block	handcuff	put into

162

B. ANSWER *Answer these questions about the story.*

1. What did Spike put on before he broke the window?
2. When did Spike break the window?
3. What happened when Spike stepped on the floor?
4. What did Spike take from the store?
5. When did Spike leave the store?
6. Did Spike run as soon as he saw the police car?
7. Where did Spike run?
8. What did the police officers do when they saw Spike?
9. What did Tina do as soon as she saw the police car?
10. What happened to Spike and Tina after the police caught them?

C. TRUE OR FALSE *Read each statement and look at the pictures. Circle **T** for **True** or **F** for **False**.*

1. Spike put on his gloves after he broke the window.   T   (F)
2. Spike climbed into the store after he broke the window.   T   F
3. As soon as Spike stepped on the floor, the police arrived.   T   F
4. Before Spike left the store, he grabbed some jewelry.   T   F
5. After he jumped out of the window, the alarm rang.   T   F
6. When he got out of the store, he heard the police siren.   T   F
7. As soon as he saw the police, he ran down an alley.   T   F
8. Before Tina could drive away, the police car blocked her.   T   F
9. Before Spike could climb over the fence, a police officer grabbed his leg.   T   F
10. After the police caught Spike, he took some jewelry.   T   F

D. COMPLETE *Complete these sentences about the story.*

1. Spike _put on a mask_____ before he got out of the car.

2. Spike _____ before he climbed into the store.

3. When Spike stepped on the floor, _____ .

4. After Spike heard the alarm, _____ .

5. Spike _____ after he took the jewelry.

6. As soon as Spike saw the police car, he _____ .

7. When Tina saw the police, _____ .

8. Spike ran down an alley when _____ .

9. A police officer _____ before he could climb over the fence.

10. After Spike and Tina were caught, the police _____ .

Working Together

A. DISCUSSION *Discuss these questions in a small group.*

1. Were you or someone in your family ever the victim of a crime? Tell your classmates about it.
2. Did you ever witness a crime? Tell what happened.
3. Is crime a problem in your city or town?
4. Are law enforcement agencies doing anything special about crime where you live?
5. Do people in your area worry about robberies? What do they do to prevent them?
6. Do you worry about a robbery?
7. How do you keep your valuables safe?

B. ON THE SUBWAY *Sit in a group and write a short description of this crime. Be sure to use* **when, after** *and* **as soon as** *in your story. Write an ending to the story.*

C. STUDENT TO STUDENT

Student A: *Student B will ask you ten questions about the subway robbery. Listen and circle the correct answer below.*
Student B: *Turn to page 187.*

1. a. before he got on the subway   b. as soon as he got on the subway

2. a. before Mr. Brown got on the subway   b. after Mr. Brown got on the subway

3. a. before Mr. Brown got on the subway   b. after Mr. Brown got on the subway

4. a. before Mr. Brown fell asleep   b. as soon as Mr. Brown fell asleep

5. a. before Joe tried to take the money   b. as soon as Joe tried to take the money

6. a. before Kathy yelled   b. as soon as Kathy yelled

7. a. before he got off the subway   b. after he got off the subway

8. a. before Kathy yelled   b. as soon as Kathy yelled

9. a. before Joe ran away   b. after Joe ran away

10. a. before Joe ran away   b. after Joe ran away

■ D. HOW SAFE ARE YOU? *Review present time clauses. Complete each sentence; then compare your answers with a classmate's.*

1. Before I leave my home, I _____.

2. Before I go on a vacation, I _____.

3. As soon as I enter my house, I _____.

4. When I have a lot of cash in my house, I _____.

5. When I am at an ATM,* I _____.

6. Before I get into my car at night, I _____.

7. As soon as I get into my car, I always _____.

8. When I walk alone at night, I always _____.

*ATM—automatic teller machine

■ A. STORY *Read the story and answer the questions.*

The Booking

After the police arrived at the police station with Spike and Tina, they had a lot of procedures to complete. First, they put Spike's and Tina's names into a computer. A nationwide service called NCIC (National Crime Information Center) has computerized information on all criminals. The police wanted to find out if Spike and Tina were using their real names, and they also wanted to know if they had been in trouble before. There was no information on Tina, but the police found out that Spike had been arrested two years ago for burglary.

Then the police took Tina's and Spike's fingerprints. They kept one copy of prints for their own police department and sent one copy to the state and another copy to the FBI.

After the police took their prints, they took pictures of Spike and Tina for the files. Before Spike and Tina signed the fingerprints form, the police reread them their rights. After the police were sure that they understood their rights, Tina and Spike signed the forms. Their signatures were also useful as handwriting samples.

When Spike and Tina finished signing the forms, the police told them to empty their pockets and to remove their belts and shoelaces. Spike and Tina were both allowed to make one telephone call. When Spike called his lawyer, he heard his lawyer's answering machine, so the police allowed him to make a second call. Tina called her mother.

Because it was late at night and the court was closed until the next morning, Tina and Spike had to spend the night in jail. The next morning, a judge set bail for Spike and Tina. Spike didn't use any weapons in the burglary, so the judge set his bail at $1000. Tina's bail was set at $750. Tina's mother paid her bail, and Spike's lawyer arranged to pay 10% of his bail. They promised to appear in court in two weeks.

1. Why did the police check the NCIC?

   _____

2. Was this Spike's first arrest?

   _____

3. What did the police do after they checked the NCIC?

   _____

4. How many copies of fingerprints did the police take?

   _____

5. What did the police do after they took Spike's and Tina's prints?

   _____

6. What did Spike and Tina do when they finished signing the forms?

_____

7. When did Spike call his lawyer?

_____

8. Why did the police allow Spike to make another call?

_____

9. Why did they have to spend the night in jail?

_____

10. When will they appear in court?

_____

■ B. SENTENCE COMBINING *Combine each pair of sentences with a past time clause using the word in parentheses. Change repeated subjects to pronouns.*

1. The police arrived at the police station. The police had many procedures to complete. (when)

   When the police arrived at the police station, they had many procedures to complete.

2. The police arrested Spike and Tina. The police took Spike and Tina to the police station. (after)

   _____

3. The police brought Spike and Tina to the police station. The police checked their background. (after)

   _____

4. The police took fingerprints. The police made three copies. (when)

   _____

5. Spike and Tina listened carefully. The police reread Spike and Tina their rights. (when)

   _____

6. The police gave them permission. They made phone calls. (after)

   _____

7. Spike's lawyer didn't answer. Spike called his brother. (when)

   _____

8. They spent a night in jail. They talked to a judge. (after)

_____

9. The judge released Spike and Tina. The judge made Spike and Tina pay bail. (before)

_____

Sharing Our Stories

Read Naomi's story about a neighborhood crime.

Many years ago, my grandparents and a neighbor were talking in the living room. My grandfather was looking through the window, and he saw a truck in the street. Ten minutes later, he saw two men. They were putting furniture in the truck. So he asked my grandmother and the neighbor, "Are Maria and Pablo going to move?"

As soon as the neighbor saw the men, she said, "They're thieves!"

My grandfather went out of the house and got into his old car, and Lidia, the neighbor, took the broom and got into the car, too. My grandmother stayed in the house.

My grandfather and Lidia went after the thieves, but the thieves' truck was faster than my grandfather's car, so they didn't catch them.

When the owners of the house came back from the beach, my grandfather said, "I'm sorry. I saw what happened, but I couldn't stop them. My car is too old."

Maria and Pablo said, "Fortunately, you didn't catch the thieves. Don't worry. The insurance will pay for everything and more."

My grandfather was surprised. He said, "I will never risk my life again for problems which aren't mine."

Naomi Ortiz

 Write a description of a crime that happened to you or to a family member or friend. When and where did it happen? Describe the crime. Was anyone hurt? Did the police investigate? Did they ever catch the criminal?

Having Fun with the Language

■ **A. BEFORE AND AFTER** *Choose six of the phrases on page 169. Use **before** or **after** and write about an event in your life. Share your sentences with a partner.*

EXAMPLE

came to the United States → Before I came to the United States, I got a visa.

came to the United States	got married	graduated from high school
had a baby	fell in love	entered college
became a citizen	found an apartment	got my driver's license
bought a house	got a pet	learned how to use a computer

■ B. SAFETY PATROL
Look at each situation. What's the problem? How can these people improve their safety?

■ C. LOCAL POLICE BLOTTER
*Look at your local newspaper and check the local police "blotter."
A police blotter is a section of the local newspaper that lists all crimes and arrests in that area. Names, dates, and brief facts are reported. What crimes occurred in your neighborhood or in your city last week?*

Grammar Summary

■ 1. Past time clauses

A time clause begins with words such as *before, after, as soon as* and *when*. A time clause has a subject and a verb. In the past tense, both the verb in the main clause and verb in the time clause are in the past tense.

Main clause	Time clause
He began to run	**as soon as** he saw the police.

Time clause	Main clause
As soon as he saw the police,	he began to run.

Note: If the time clause is at the beginning of the sentence, use a comma to separate it from the main clause.

18 The Power Went Out

Past Continuous

A. LISTEN: THE POWER WENT OUT *Look at the picture and listen to the story about the effects of the power blackout in the city. Draw a line from the name of each person or persons to their location when the power went out.*

Past Continuous		
I		
He	was	
She		
It		eating dinner.
You		
We	were	
They		

- The Wilsons
- Becky
- Susan and Frank
- Mike Tanaka
- Officer Rodriguez

Where was each person when the power went out? What was each person doing?

◼ B. CHECKING THE FACTS *Read each sentence about the blackout and circle **Yes** or **No**.*

1.	It was a cool evening.	Yes	No
2.	The power went out at 9:00.	Yes	No
3.	The Wilsons were watching TV.	Yes	No
4.	Becky was playing softball.	Yes	No
5.	Susan and her husband were celebrating his birthday.	Yes	No
6.	Mike Tanaka was working at his office.	Yes	No
7.	Officer Rodriguez was driving around in his patrol car when the power went out.	Yes	No

◼ C. PAST CONTINUOUS *Complete these sentences with the verb in the past tense or the past continuous tense. Not every sentence needs a past continuous verb!*

> **Past Continuous**
>
> The past continuous describes a continuous action in the past.
>
> The past tense describes an action that interrupted or stopped the action.
>
> | **Main** clause | **Time** clause |
> |---|---|
> | They were eating | **when** the power went out. |
> | He was copying a report | **when** the power died. |

1. Becky _____ (play) softball when the lights _____ (go) out.

2. When the lights _____ (go) out, Becky's team _____ (win).

3. Becky _____ (stand) on first base.

4. When the lights _____ (go) out, the coach _____ (call) the power company.

5. After they _____ (wait) for a half an hour, everyone _____ (leave).

6. Mike Tanaka _____ (work) late at his office with his staff when the power _____ (die).

7. The staff _____ (try) to finish an important project.

8. Mike _____ (print) a report when the machine _____ (stop).

9. Everyone _____ (be) tired, and they _____ (be) glad to go home.

10. Everyone _____ (have) to walk down the steps because the elevator _____ (work).

■ D. ANSWER *Answer the questions about each of the pictures.*

1.

    a. Where were Susan and Frank?
    b. What were they celebrating?
    c. Did they go home when the power went out?
    d. What did the waiters do?

2.

    a. Where were the Wilsons?
    b. What were they doing?
    c. How long did they wait before they went home?

3.

    a. Where was Officer Rodriguez?
    b. What was he doing when the lights went out?
    c. What did he do then?

Working Together

■ A. DISCUSSION *Sit in a small group and discuss these questions.*

1. Did the power ever go out in your city or town?
2. When did it happen?
3. What caused the power blackout?
4. What were you doing when the power went out?
5. What did you do next?
6. How long did you wait before the power came back on?
7. Did the power blackout affect the whole neighborhood?

B. THE NEIGHBORHOOD

Ask and answer questions about what the people in this neighborhood were doing when the power went out.

1.

   What was Jack doing when the power went out?
   What was he watching?
   What did he do when the television went out?

2.

   What was Carolyn doing when the power went out?
   What was she working on?
   What did she do when her computer turned off?

3.

   What was Nancy doing when the power went out?
   What was she buying?
   What did the manager do when the lights went out in the store?
   How did the children feel?

4.

   What was Steve doing when the power went out?
   Where was he?
   What did he do when the machines stopped working?

C. STUDENT TO STUDENT

Student A: *You are a police officer, and you just stopped* **Student B,** *a driver. Ask the questions below about the traffic incident. Listen for the answers. Practice the conversation several times until you can say it comfortably.*

Student B: *Turn to page 188 and give the correct answer.*

Student A: (Police Officer)

1. Did you see the stop sign?
2. Why weren't you paying attention?
3. Why were you driving so fast?
4. Where were you going?

Stay on the same page, but change roles. Student B is now the police officer.

Student A: *You were driving when* **Student B,** *a police officer, stopped you. Listen to the questions and give the correct answer from these responses. Practice the conversation several times until you can say it comfortably.*

Student A: (Driver)

No, I didn't. I was listening to the radio.

I was looking at a map, so I didn't see it.

My friend is getting married, and I was trying to get to the wedding.

Really? I was speeding?

A few pairs of students should volunteer to role play one of the situations for the class.

Practicing on Your Own

A. MATCHING HALVES *Match the ideas in the sentence halves; then write a complete sentence. Use a different name for the subject of each sentence.*

_C_ 1. play baseball	a. cut/finger with a knife
_____ 2. drive to work	b. power go out
_____ 3. shop at the mall	c. fall and break/ankle
_____ 4. cut vegetables	d. burn/finger
_____ 5. walk home from school	e. see an accident
_____ 6. watch TV	f. begin to rain
_____ 7. cook dinner	g. meet a friend

Richard was playing baseball when he fell and broke his ankle.

B. SENTENCE COMPLETION *Complete these sentences. Use the correct tense, past or past continuous.*

1. I was watching TV when _____ .

2. I was walking down the street when _____ .

3. We were _____ when we saw the accident.

4. I was going to work when _____ .

5. I _____ when I heard the news.

6. I _____ when the storm began.

7. We were _____ when _____ .

8. When _____ , I was _____ .

C. THE POPE COMES TO NEW YORK *Read this story about the Pope's visit to New York City.*

Mary Frances O'Reilly was very excited. She was sitting with her family in Central Park in New York City. She had driven all the way from North Carolina for a special event—the Pope was coming for a visit, and she was going to see him for the first time! She was sitting with her grandmother, two of her sisters, and her three children. They were sitting in the tenth row, so they were going to get a good look at everything. Mary Frances was thinking about all the good stories she could tell her friends. She also had four rolls of film to create permanent memories of the visit.

Central Park was full of all kinds of people. They were all waiting expectantly for the Pope. There were many vendors with booths nearby. The vendors were selling T-shirts, mugs, hats, postcards, and many other souvenirs of the Pope's visit. A choir was practicing their songs. Several priests were preparing the stage.

When the Pope finally arrived, everyone clapped and shouted. Security officers were running next to the car, looking at the crowds and protecting the Pope. People were standing on chairs to get a better look. Many Frances was taking a lot of pictures. When the Pope rode by in his Popemobile, he was waving at the crowd.

During the Mass, people were praying. Some people were holding up posters. Some were watching the large video screens. Others were listening to the Mass on the radio, too. Mostly, the park was quiet and calm. Everyone was listening to the Pope.

Complete the dialogue between a reporter and Mary Frances. Use the information in the story and your own ideas about the events of the day.

1. Interviewer: What were you thinking about before the Pope arrived?

   Mary Frances: I was thinking about all the good stories I could tell.

2. Interviewer: What was happening in the park while everyone was waiting?

   Mary Frances: _____

3. Interviewer: What kind of souvenirs were they selling?

   Mary Frances: _____

4. Interviewer: Was anyone singing?

   Mary Frances: _____

5. Interviewer: What did everyone do when the Pope finally arrived?

   Mary Frances: _____

6. Interviewer: Were there many security officers? What were they doing?

   Mary Frances: _____

7. Interviewer: What were you doing while the Pope was going to the stage?

   Mary Frances: _____

8. Interviewer: What was the atmosphere during the Mass?

   Mary Frances: _____

Having Fun with the Language

A. OBSERVATIONS *In small groups of three students, go to a common area in your school, such as the library, cafeteria, front lobby, front steps, or student lounge. Stay there for three to five minutes. Then come back to your classmates and report on what was happening in the area that you observed.*

B. VIDEO *Watch five minutes of an action scene from a movie. Take a few notes while you are watching. Then, in groups, write a short paragraph about the scene, trying to use the past continuous tense and* **when** *clauses. Suggested movies:* Home Alone, The Fugitive, Stripes.

Grammar Summary

1. Past continuous statements

I He She	was	watching TV.
We You They	were	playing ball.

2. Time clauses: *when* statements

Use the past continuous to describe a continuous action in the past.

Use the simple past to describe the action that interrupted or stopped the action.

Main clause	Time clause
They were watching a movie	**when** the power went out.

Time clause	Main clause
When the power went out,	they were watching a movie.

Note: If the time clause is at the beginning of the sentence, use a comma to separate it from the main clause.

Appendix

Irregular Past Verbs

be	was/were	fly	flew	say	said
bear	bore	forget	forgot	see	saw
become	became	get	got	sell	sold
begin	began	give	gave	send	sent
bite	bit	go	went	set	set
break	broke	hang	hung	sing	sang
bring	brought	have	had	sit	sat
buy	bought	hear	heard	sleep	slept
catch	caught	hold	held	speak	spoke
choose	chose	hurt	hurt	speed	sped
come	came	keep	kept	spend	spent
cost	cost	know	knew	stand	stood
cut	cut	leave	left	stick	stuck
do	did	let	let	swim	swam
draw	drew	lose	lost	take	took
drink	drank	make	made	teach	taught
drive	drove	meet	met	tell	told
eat	ate	pay	paid	think	thought
fall	fell	put	put	understand	understood
feed	fed	read	read	wake	woke
feel	felt	ride	rode	wear	wore
fight	fought	ring	rang	win	won
find	found	run	ran	write	wrote

Student to Student Exercises

Unit 1, page 8

Student B: *Use the chart below.*
Student A: *Turn to page 8.*

You both have a chart of four workers, but some of the information is missing. Ask and answer questions to complete your charts.

Who is a _____ ?
What is _____ ?
What's his/her address?
What floor is his/her office on?
What's his/her office number?

	Job	Address	Floor	Office
Mrs. Baker	Real estate agent		second	
	Lawyer	893 Forest Avenue	tenth	
Mr. Davis	Engineer	647 Bay Drive		
Ms. Wilson		155 River Road		
Mr. Perez	Computer analyst		fourth	416

Unit 2, page 19

Student A: *Look at page 19.*
Student B: *Student A will ask you seven questions about the average American* **man.** *Look below and answer the question with the correct information.*

72
162 pounds

$28,500
5 feet, 9 inches
26

12
9 1/2 C

When you finish, change pages. **Student B** *will ask questions about the average American* **woman.** **Student A** *will look below and answer the questions with the correct information.*

80
135 pounds

$17,000
5 feet, 4 inches
24

18
7 1/2 B

Unit 3, page 30

Ask and answer questions about how these people commute to work in Chicago. Complete the chart.
Student A: *Look at the chart on page 31.*
Student B: *Look at the chart below.*

> **EXAMPLE**
>
> Where does Amy live?
>
> How does she get to work?
>
> How long does it take her?

	Town	Transportation	Time
Amy			
Brian	Naperville	Metro train	45 minutes
Lisa and Silvia			
Matthew and Ed	Evanston	car	25 minutes

Unit 4, page 43

Student B *will look at the chart below, and* **Student A** *will look at the chart on page 43. You each have different facts about the largest state, Alaska. Ask and answer questions with* **How much** *or* **How many** *and complete the information in your chart.*

> **EXAMPLE**
>
> **Student A:** How many islands are there in Alaska?
>
> **Student B:** There are 1,800 islands.

Alaska	
islands	1,800
volcanoes	
glaciers	100,000
lakes	
rivers	3,000
national parks	

snowfall	20 feet (northern areas)
rain	
people	610,000
Eskimos	
oil	a lot
heavy industry	
traffic	a little
fishing	

Unit 5, page 54

Ask and answer questions about the flights and fill in the missing information.

Student B: *Look at the Flight Board below.*
Student A: *Look at the Flight Board on page 55.*

EXAMPLE

When is flight 643 arriving/leaving?

What gate is it arriving at?

Which flight is going to Atlanta?

Where is Delta flight 824 going?

What gate is flight 643 arriving at?

FLIGHT BOARD

Arrivals					Departures				
Northwest	643	Chicago			Delta	449		4:10	54
Northwest	716	Toronto	4:32	45	Delta	824	Dallas		
Continental	278		6:18	67	Delta	721	Tampa	4:50	71
Continental	455	Denver			Delta	336			44

Unit 6, page 64

Student A: Read the eight sentences below to your partner.
Student B: Look at the pictures on page 64 and circle **True** *or* **False.**

Student A	Student B
1. All of the boxes are the same size.	1. Many of the boxes are the same size.
2. One of the boxes is larger than the others.	2. A couple of the boxes are gray.
3. One of the boxes is very small.	3. A few of the boxes are open.
4. Many of the boxes are black.	4. All of the boxes look alike.
5. Most of the boxes have a heart on the front.	5. None of the boxes are black.
6. One of the boxes has a ball in it.	6. None of the boxes are empty.
7. Most of the boxes are white.	7. Some of the boxes have designs on the front.
8. Some of the boxes have flowers in them.	8. A couple of the boxes have a star on the front.

When you finish, **Student B** *will read eight new sentences from the second column above.* **Student A** *will look at page 64 and circle* **True** *or* **False.**

Unit 8, page 78

The chart below gives the future plans of four people. Ask and answer questions to complete the missing information.

Student A: Turn to page 79.
Student B: Look at the chart below.

EXAMPLE

What is Yuri going to do?   He's going to travel.

Where is he going to travel?   In Europe.

	Jenny	Yuri	Amanda	Kevin
What	look for a job		go to college	
When		after his graduation		next year
Where	at the mall		in her hometown	

Unit 9, page 90

Student A: Read the ten questions below about the two largest cities in the United States.
Student B: Turn to page 90.

Student A	Student B
1. Which city has more professional sports teams?	1. Which city has a lower household income?
2. In which city is the average household income higher?	2. Which city has higher taxes?
3. Which city has lower taxes?	3. Which city has a higher expected job growth?
4. Which city has better job opportunities?	4. In which city is a house more affordable?
5. Which city has higher housing costs?	5. In which city is an apartment cheaper?
6. In which city is an apartment more expensive?	6. Which city has more hospitals?
7. Which city has more colleges?	7. Which city has more museums and art galleries?
8. Which city gets more rain?	8. Which city is drier?
9. Which city is colder in winter?	9. Which city is warmer in winter?
10. Which city is hotter in summer?	10. Which city has more varied weather?

*When you finish, **Student A** will turn to page 90. **Student B** will read the ten questions in Column B.*

Unit 11, page 106

Student A: Read the four sentences below about marriage.
*Student B: Listen and write each sentence under **I agree** or **I disagree**.*

Student A:

1. The groom should take his wife's name.
2. The bride should take her husband's name.
3. Weddings are too expensive.
4. The bride should always wear a white dress.

When you finish, change pages. **Student A** *will turn to page 106.* **Student B** *will read the four new sentences below.*

Student B:

1. Money is the most appropriate gift for a new couple.
2. The man's family should help pay for the wedding.
3. The new couple should have a will.
4. The couple should send thank-you cards for all wedding gifts.

Unit 14, page 139

Match the questions and answers.
Student A: *Turn to page 139.*
Student B: *Listen to the question and read the correct answer below.* **Student A** *will write your answer.*

Student B

To Florida.

Yes, they moved to a three-bedroom apartment.

David's brother found a good job for him.

Last summer.

When you finish, change pages. **Student B** *will ask questions 5 to 8 on page 139.* **Student A** *will read the correct answer below.*

Student A

They saw a "For Rent" sign in the window.

It was in a convenient location.

In Virginia.

No, they borrowed a friend's truck.

Unit 15, page 150

Student A: *Turn to page 150.*
Student B: *You and your partner are packing for a fishing trip tomorrow. Your partner will ask you about several items. Look below and tell your friend if you have the item or not.*

EXAMPLE

A: **Did you pack** the fishing rods?   B: Yes, I did.   *or*   No, I didn't.

A: **Did you remember** to bring the hooks?   B: No, I have to find them.

A: **How about** the worms?   B: We need to buy them in the morning.

the fishing rods   the sun block   the cooler   the net

Unit 16, page 157

Student A: Turn to page 157.

Student B: Read these five sentences about working fathers to **Student A.** Your partner will write the three sentences that he or she thinks are true.

1. There are more than one million single-father families.
2. Twenty percent of fathers watch the children when their wives go to work.
3. More mothers than fathers think companies should help employees who are parents.
4. Today, more fathers want sick leave when their children are sick.
5. Most men are not happy that their wives work.

Student A: Read these five sentences about working mothers to **Student B.** Your partner will write the three sentences that he or she thinks are true.

Student B: Turn to page 157.

1. Wives still do most of the housework at home.
2. Fifty percent of working mothers send their children to day care.
3. Less than 2% of all companies offer day care for their employees' children.
4. Most wives earn as much as their husbands.
5. Women usually feel good about their jobs when they are with other working women.

Unit 17, page 165

Student A: Turn to page 165.

Student B: Ask **Student A** the ten questions below about the story. Watch as your partner circles the answer. Do you agree with your partner's answers?

1. When did Mr. Brown cash his paycheck?
2. When did Joe get on the subway?
3. When did Kathy get on the subway?
4. When did Joe put his hand in Mr. Brown's pocket?
5. When did Kathy yell?
6. When did Mr. Brown wake up?
7. When did Joe drop the wallet?
8. When did Joe run off the subway?
9. When did Mr. Brown call the police?
10. When did Mr. Brown thank Kathy?

Student A: *Look at page 174.*

Student B: *You were driving when* **Student A,** *a police officer, stopped you.* *Listen to the questions and give the correct answer from these responses.* *Practice the conversation several times until you can say it comfortably.*

Student B: (Driver)

We were ten minutes late for our appointment.

Because my daughter was crying.

We were going to the doctor's office.

No, I didn't.

Stay on the same page, but change roles. **Student B** *is now the police officer.*

Student B: *You are a police officer, and you just stopped* **Student A,** *a driver.* *Ask the questions below about the traffic incident.* *Listen for the answers. Practice the conversation several times until you can say it comfortably.*

Student B: (Police Officer)

1. Why didn't you stop at the light?
2. Didn't you hear my siren?
3. Do you know you were speeding?
4. Why were you driving so fast?

A few pairs of students should volunteer to role play one of the situations for the class.

Tape Script

Unit 1, page 1

A. Listen: two jobs *Listen to each person talk about work. Check the words that apply to the job.*

FIRST SPEAKER

No job is perfect, and that sure is true about my job. My name is Susan, and I'm a parking meter reader. I walk along the street and around the parking lots in town. If a parking meter reads VIOLATION, I give the vehicle a ticket. In this town, the fine for overtime parking is ten dollars.

How do I like my job? I like some things, but not others. First, no one likes to see me. When drivers see me writing a ticket, they usually say nothing, but they aren't exactly friendly. Some drivers get angry or say bad things to me. Look, I'm only doing my job. Another problem is the weather. I work outside in all kinds of weather—hot, cold, rain, snow. And after a few hours walking, my legs get tired. The work is easy, but it isn't interesting; it's the same thing over and over. I just write license plate numbers.

But my job isn't all bad. The hours are great, from 9:00 to 5:00, five days a week. There are no evening hours, so I can be home with my family. My job is close to home, in the next town. And I'm a city employee. My salary is ten dollars an hour, and I have medical benefits and three weeks' vacation. I'm not crazy about my job, but I'm staying.

SECOND SPEAKER

My name is Rosa, and I'm a small business owner. I have a florist shop near my home. Part of the business is walk-in; people pick up flowers or plants for their homes or their friends. But the biggest part of the business is special occasions. Flowers say "Congratulations," and flowers say "I'm sorry." People need flowers for weddings, parties, and funerals.

I love my job, especially making special flower arrangements. The work isn't difficult, but it's creative and it's different every day. The customers are always friendly and happy with our work.

But it's difficult to own your own business. When the florist shop is busy, the hours are long, and I work on weekends. When you own your own business, you pay for your feel relaxed. But when business is slow, I worry about paying the bills. When you own your own business, you pay for your own benefits. I have medical insurance, and it's difficult to take a vacation, too.

page 5

G. Listen: numbers *Listen and complete each sentence with the number you hear.*

1. He works on the ninth floor.
2. He's in room 947.
3. Her address is 629 Maple Avenue.
4. She's on the fifth floor, in apartment 539.
5. They work at 667 North Union Avenue.
6. She works in the Medical Building, at 244 Spring Street.
7. Her office is on the third floor, in room 313.
8. I was on the sixth floor last year, but now I'm on the seventh floor in room 719.
9. The address is 486 Treemont Drive.
10. She is at 297 Weston Avenue.

Unit 2, page 15

B. Listen: Charlie *Listen to Charlie describe himself and his lifestyle. You will need to take a few notes. Compare Charlie to the average American male.*

Hi. My name is Charlie Johnson, and I'm supposed to tell you a little about myself. OK. I'm 32 years old and I'm single, yup, a bachelor, never got married, and I don't know if I ever will. I'm 6'2" tall, and I'm about 210 pounds. I guess I could lose a little weight. I'm a computer programmer at a small company. I really like my job; it's interesting, and my co-workers are great. I earn a good salary, $43,000 this year, but I work hard, usually ten hours a day, sometimes more if we're working on some big project. I live here in the city, in a one-bedroom apartment. I like it because it's near a lot of good restaurants and I can walk to work. And, let's see, I have a pet fish, Goldie. I'd like a dog, but I don't really have time to walk one and take care of one, so it's just me and Goldie.

Unit 3, page 26

A. Listen: getting to school *Listen and write the name of each person and the number of minutes it takes to get to school.*

School begins at 9:00. Some students live close to school and walk only a few blocks. Others commute from ten, twenty, and thirty miles.

Ali and George: Ali and George live close to school in Newark, and they walk together every morning. It takes them only five minutes.

David: David lives the farthest from school in Plainfield. He takes the bus to school in the morning. It takes him 40 minutes.

Ann: Ann has an easy drive because she lives in the next town, Cranford. She drives to school, and it takes her 15 minutes.

Susan and Paul: Susan and Paul live in Linden, only a mile from school, but they drive. The traffic is always heavy, and it takes them 10 minutes.

Patty: Patty doesn't have a car, but she is saving for one. Every morning, Patty lives in Morristown. She takes the train to Newark, then walks a few blocks to school. It takes her about 30 minutes to get to school.

Lee: Lee has a car, but he doesn't drive. He wants to stay in shape, so he rides his bicycle to school. It takes him 25 minutes, and he thinks it's great exercise. When it rains, he drives.

page 27

C. Listen: Questions *Listen and write the question you hear. Circle the correct answer.*

1. Where does Patty live?
2. How does she get to school?
3. How long does it take her?
4. Where do Ali and George live?
5. How do they get to school?
6. How long does it take them?

Now listen to two personal questions. Write the question and your answer.

7. How do you get to school?
8. How long does it take you?

Unit 4, page 36

A. Listen: Georgia *Listen to a description of Georgia. As you listen, write the number of each feature, location, or product in the circles on the map below.*

Georgia lies in the southeastern part of the United States. It is the largest state east of the Mississippi. It is bordered by South Carolina on the northeast, North Carolina and Tennessee on the north, Alabama on the west, and Florida on the south. The Atlantic Ocean forms Georgia's eastern border. The climate is mild, with hot and humid summers and cool, wet winters.

The northern part of the state is an area of mountains, valleys, and rivers. The Appalachian Mountains and the Blue Ridge Mountains run through the northern part of the state.

The central part of the state is a plateau, a high area of both flat land and rolling hills. This central area is the most popu-lated part of the state, and it contains many of Georgia's largest cities and much of Georgia's industry. Atlanta, the capital, lies in the northwestern part of this plateau. It's a major city, the home of Coca-Cola and CNN News.

A coastal plain covers the southern part of the state. This area offers rich farmland for crops such as peanuts, tobacco, and corn. Peanuts are one of the state's most important products. Half of the peanut butter eaten in the United States is made from Georgia peanuts. Georgia's nickname is the Peach State because so many peaches grow there.

The Okefenokee Swamp lies at the bottom of Georgia. The swamp is the home of alligators, deer, black bears, and rare birds. Very few people live in this area. Most of the swamp is a wildlife refuge.

page 37

B. Listen: Singular or plural Circle the letter of the noun you hear.

1. mountains	7. peaches
2. city	8. state
3. peanuts	9. industry
4. area	10. birds
5. summer	11. class
6. homes	12. people

page 40

G. Listen: Montana Look at this feature map of Montana and listen to the description. Complete the sentences by circling *is* or *are*, then use one of the quantifiers from the boxes below.

Montana is the fourth largest state in the United States. It is located in the northern part of the United States, sharing a border with Canada. Montana is divided into two geographic areas. The Rocky Mountains take up the western one-third of Montana. The Great Plains cover the eastern two-thirds of the state. Several major rivers run through Montana, both in the Rockies and in the Great Plains. The Missouri River, the second longest river in the U.S., begins in Montana.

Because Montana is so far north, its winter are cold, often with heavy snowstorms. The western part of the state receives a lot of rain. But the Rocky Mountains block the rain clouds, and the rain often does not make it over the mountains and into the valleys on the east. The Great Plains are drier, and the summers are very hot.

With fewer than one million inhabitants, Montana has one of the lowest populations in the United States, only 800,000 people. Of these, about 50,000 are Native Americans. Most of the Indians live on the state's seven Indian reservations, but many live in the towns and cities throughout the state. Towns and cities are small and far apart.

The Rocky Mountains and the Great Plains determine Montana's industries. The Rockies are an area of heavy forests, helping to make the lumber business one of Montana's leading industries. Montana is a mining state. Oil and coal are Montana's most valuable minerals. Miners also dig for gold, silver, and copper in the Rocky Mountains. Tourism is one of the state's leading industries. Thousands of tourists visit Glacier National Park each summer and fall to enjoy the spectacular hik-ing and riding trails and to view the more than 50 active glaciers. Mountain climbers and backpackers enjoy climbing the Rockies. In winter, skiers speed down the snow-covered slopes. Fishing is popular in Montana's many rivers and lakes. The Great Plains are the home of Montana's ranches and farms. Cattle and sheep ranches produce beef, milk, and wool, and Montana's farmers grow wheat, hay, barley, and potatoes.

Unit 5, page 50

A. Listen: the airport *Listen and write each name under the correct picture.*

It's a weekday morning, and the airport isn't crowded. The plane for Detroit is boarding, and most people are already on the plane. Charles is boarding the plane. He's pulling a carry-on suitcase. Ben is handing his ticket to the flight attendant.

Kathy and Lisa are sisters, they are saying good-bye to each other.

Another flight attendant is checking tickets and assigning seats. Mark is at the counter now. He's asking for a window seat, if possible.

There are several people waiting for the next flight to Chicago. Brian has a meeting at 1:00 this afternoon. He's relaxing and reading the newspaper. Jessica is standing at the window with her daughter. They're watching the planes land. Amanda owns a small import business. She's using her computer to check on sales. Chris is very tired because he was up with his friends until late last night. He's sleeping. Megan is relaxing and listening to her tape player. John is calling his wife in Chicago. He's asking her to meet him at the airport.

page 52

E. Listen: Questions *Listen and write the question you hear. Then circle the correct answer.*

1. Where is Mark standing?
2. Who is he talking to?
3. What is he asking for?
4. Where are Jessica and her daughter standing?
5. What are they looking at?

Unit 6, page 61

A. Listen: the classroom *Listen to these sentences about the classroom. Circle **True** or **False**.*

1. Everyone is in class today.
2. No one is in class today.
3. Someone is absent.
4. No one is absent.
5. Someone is standing.
6. Everyone is sitting down.
7. No one is drinking soda.
8. Everyone is smoking.
9. Everyone is writing on the blackboard.
10. Someone is writing on the blackboard.
11. No one is writing on the blackboard.
12. Someone is speaking.
13. No one is speaking.
14. Everyone is speaking.
15. Everyone is studying English.

Unit 7, page 68

A. Listen: requests *Listen to each request. Write the number of the request in the box next to each person's name.*

1. Can I get a drink of water?   Wait until after class, please.
2. Could I borrow an eraser?   Of course.
3. Could I get a book from the library?   Wait until break time, please.
4. Can I sharpen my pencil?   Yes, you can.
5. Could you lend me a quarter?   Sure. Here.

Unit 8, page 72

A. Listen: future plans *Today is graduation at Central High School. Listen to each student's plans; then write his or her name under the correct picture.*

1. Brian is the captain of the high school baseball team. He's a great player. He's going to sign a contract with a professional baseball team.
2. Lisa is going to work in her parents' travel agency. She's going to take some courses in business part time.
3. Alex is going to take cooking classes in a college in the city and work in a restaurant.

4. Tom is going to go to college in another state. He thinks he's going to study computer programming.

5. Dan is going to join the army. He's leaving for basic training in July.

6. Sally is in love. She's going to get married in August.

7. Diana is going to attend the local community college and study for her LPN degree.

8. Kelly wants to see the world. She's going to travel around Europe with a friend this summer. In September, she's going to go to college.

page 75

D. Listen: present and present continuous with future meaning The school newspaper is interviewing two graduating seniors about their future plans. Listen to the interviews; then answer the questions.

Conversation 1

Reporter: We're interviewing students for the school newspaper. What are your plans after graduation?

Dan: I'm going to join the army.

Reporter: Great! Did you already enlist?

Dan: Yes. I leave for basic training in Virginia on July 15th. Basic training is 12 weeks. In October I start technical training in mechanics.

Reporter: Are you going to stay in the army for two or for four years?

Dan: At least four years.

Reporter: Good luck.

Conversation 2

Reporter: We're talking to some of the graduates and asking them about their plans for the future.

Sally: I'm getting married.

Reporter: Congratulations! Can you tell me about your plans?

Sally: We're getting married August 1st. Then we're taking a one-week honeymoon to the Florida Keys.

Reporter: And after that? Will you continue your education?

Sally: Yes. I'm going to work and go to school part time. I have a part-time job now in a doctor's office. I'm going to work there full time and go to school two nights a week.

Reporter: Best of luck.

Sally: Thank you.

Unit 9, page 88

F. Listen: The Best Places to Live Every year in its July issue, Money magazine rates the best places to live in the United States. In 1996, the top two cities were Madison, Wisconsin, and Punta Gorda, Florida. Find these two states on the map inside the back cover. Listen to the information about these cities and complete the chart.

Madison, Wisconsin, is a small city in the southern part of the state. The residents of this city believe their community is active and friendly, with a strong economy, great health care, and a large variety of recreational activities. The population is almost 400,000. The unemployment rate is one of the lowest in the United States, only 1.5%. And the cost of a house is very reasonable. A family can buy a comfortable three-bedroom home for $123,000. The property taxes for a typical house are $3,800 a year, and the state sales tax is 5.5%. Parents say that the schools are excellent, and most of the children in Madison attend the public schools. One complaint about Madison is the weather. There are 190 sunny days a year, but the winter is cold, averaging about 20°. The average summer temperature is a comfortable 70°.

Punta Gorda, Florida, is located in southern Florida on the west coast, on the Gulf of Mexico. The population is only 125,000, but the town continues to grow at a fast rate. The economy of Punta Gorda is growing, too, with only a 4.6% unemployment rate. Punta Gorda has a high proportion of senior citizens, about 35%, but younger families are coming to the area, attracted by the weather, the beautiful beaches, the job opportunities, and the relaxed, small town atmosphere. A typical three-bedroom house is about $165,000, and the taxes on the typical home are a low $1,700. The sales tax is 7% on most items. The schools are rated as average. The weather is one of Florida's star attractions. It is sunny 264 days a year. The average temperature in the summer is over 90°; in the winter, the temperature is more comfortable, in the 60's and 70's.

A. Listen: Learning English *Gloria began to study English two months ago. Listen to her speak about herself and about learning to speak English; then circle* **can** *or* **can't** *in each sentence.*

Hi. My name is Gloria. I came to the United States 10 years ago. You say, 10 years ago?! And you don't speak English well?

I came to the United States when I was 25. And the next year I had another child. My little boy was only 5. She was born here, in Miami. So I stayed home. I live in a Spanish neighborhood. All my friends are here, and we speak Spanish all day. I can watch TV in Spanish, and I can listen to the news in Spanish. In the stores, the clerks can speak Spanish. There's even a Spanish teller at the bank, so I can speak Spanish with her.

So I can only speak a little English. In class, I can understand the teacher. I can read the book and answer the questions. I can understand all the grammar exercises. But when I try to use my English, I have big problems. I can follow people if they speak slowly. I try to answer, but I need time to think. And I can't ask questions easily.

I want to improve my English. I want to practice more. But how? I can't practice with my neighbors because they don't speak English. And my kids just smile when I try to speak with them. What can I do?

page 98

C. Listen: pronunciation *Listen to these sentences about Gloria and her children. Circle* **can** *or* **can't.** *Then read the sentences to a partner.*

> Note the difference in the sound of a.
> They can speak English.
> They can't speak English.

1. Gloria's children can speak English.
2. They can speak Spanish, too.
3. Her son can read Spanish.
4. Her daughter can't read Spanish.
5. She can only read English.
6. Gloria can't speak English with her children.
7. She can't speak with their teachers, either.
8. She can't help them with their homework.

Unit 11, page 103

A. Listen: wedding plans *Michael and Patty just got engaged. It's January, and they plan to get married in August. Listen to the timetable for some of their plans, and match the month and the item.*

Michael and Patty just got engaged. It's January, and they plan to get married in August. In the United States, most weddings take place in the bride's hometown. So, first, they have to talk to the minister at Patty's church to set an exact date for the wedding. In February, they are going to look at several restaurants and halls and decide where to have the reception. It takes several months to make the wedding gown, so Patty has to choose and order a wedding gown in March. In April, they have to look at rings at several jewelers and choose their wedding rings. During May, they have to talk to both families, they make up the final guest list, and order the right number of invitations. They have to send the invitations in late June. The month before the wedding, Patty and Michael have to have their blood tests and get the marriage license. In August, they have to go over all the arrangements carefully to be sure that everything is ready for the wedding and reception.

page 104

A. Listen: decisions, decisions *Patty and Michael have a lot to decide about their wedding and reception. Listen to their conversation and answer these questions.*

Michael: Let's keep the reception reasonable. I don't want a big wedding, something small, not too much money.

Patty: That sounds fine to me. But how are we going to limit the guest list? Maybe we should just invite brothers and sisters, aunts and uncles. No cousins, no children.

Michael: But I have to invite my cousins!

President. In 1993, Bill Clinton, a Democrat, became president.

He was in office for two terms and left office in 1989. The Republicans stayed in power, and George Bush became the next lost to Ronald Reagan. Reagan, a Republican and conservative, was the oldest president in the history of the United States. the next Democratic president and was elected in 1976 and took office in 1977. He was a one-term president. In 1980, he scandal. Ford, his vice president, became president and finished his term. Ford was president until 1977. Jimmy Carter was from 1969 to 1974. He did not serve two full terms. Nixon was the only president to resign from office because of a political Johnson, who was the vice president, became president and then won one more term. He, too, was a Democrat. Nixon was president Lyndon Johnson, who was the vice president, became president and then won one more term. He, too, was a Democrat. Nixon was president from 1963 to 1969. The next two presidents, Nixon and Ford, were Republicans.

elected to office. Kennedy served as president only from 1961 to 1963 because he was shot and killed in Dallas, Texas.

In 1961, John F. Kennedy, a Democrat, was elected president of the United States. He was the youngest president ever

year term.) *Under* **Party,** *write* **D** *for Democrat or* **R** *for Republican.*

B. Listen: the presidents—1961 to present *Listen and write the years of each president's term.* (*A president is elected for a four-*

Unit 13, page 123

10. Which car would be the most practical for you and your family?

9. Which car is the most economical?

8. Which car is the best for a large family?

7. Which car gets the best gas mileage?

6. Which car is the easiest to park?

5. Which car is the safest in snow?

4. Which car is the smallest?

3. Which car carries the most passengers?

2. Which car is the cheapest?

1. Which car is the most expensive?

A. Listen: which car? *Listen to the questions and check the answers.*

Unit 12, page 112

Patty: OK. Let's look around.

the middle, somewhere between Austin and San Antonio?

Michael: I know, but most of my family is here, in San Antonio. For the reception, maybe we should look for a place in

there, too.

Patty: I know. But weddings are almost always in the bride's town. My whole family lives there. And your sister lives

Michael: But that's 75 miles from here.

Patty: Michael, I want to get married in a church, in St. Mark's in Austin. I've been a member of St. Mark's my whole life!

rant or a hall?

Michael: You're right—inside. Should we have the wedding ceremony and the reception in the same place, in a restau-

Patty: And what will we do if it rains?

Michael: Yes, that's good. The weather is usually nicer. I know—let's get married outside!

Patty: We'll never be ready by the spring. We need more time for planning. How about this summer, in August?

Michael: When should we get married, this spring or this summer?

Patty: We can forget about your idea for a small wedding.

Michael: It's more like thirty.

Patty: Don't you have about twenty cousins?

Unit 14, page 130

A. Listen: the move Miguel and Ana just moved into a new apartment. Listen to the story and number the pictures from 1 to 6.

Miguel and Ana were unhappy in their last apartment. The rent was low, but the area was unsafe. There were often robberies, and someone broke into their last apartment last month. They looked in the newspaper, talked to friends, and drove around areas that they liked, and finally found a nice apartment in a two-family house. They signed a lease and paid a security deposit. Miguel and Ana packed all their clothes and books and kitchen things in boxes. Before they moved, the landlord painted the apartment and changed the locks. On the first of the month, Miguel and Ana borrowed a van, and friends helped them move in.

page 131

C. Listen: pronunciation Listen to these past tense verbs. Write the number of syllables you hear in each verb. Repeat the verbs.

1. changed	5. painted	9. carried
2. rented	6. helped	10. wanted
3. looked	7. called	11. lived
4. needed	8. started	12. fixed

page 133

B. Listen: finding an apartment Put your pencil down and listen twice to Miguel and Ana's story about finding their new apartment. Then try to complete the story with the verbs from Exercise A.

We were lucky in finding our current apartment. Before this, we lived in a different town, but we weren't happy there. The area wasn't safe, and last month someone broke into our apartment and stole our TV and stereo. We talked to friends and looked in the paper, but we didn't find anything. Then one day we got in the car and drove around in a neighborhood we both liked. We were on a quiet street a few blocks from town when we saw a two-family house with a sign in the window, "Apartment for Rent, Inquire Within." We rang the doorbell. The owner was home, and he showed us around the apartment. It was sunny and clean with lots of room. We signed a lease that day and paid him one month's rent and a security deposit. We were very lucky! The owner told us, "I just put the sign in the window this morning!"

page 136

C. Listen: Chin-Hao's story Chin-Hao is a young man from China. Listen to his story and take notes.

Chin-Hao came to the United States in 1992, when he was 23 years old. He didn't speak English. He lived with his uncle for a year, but the house was small and crowded. He finally found a job in a shoe factory and saved a little money. In 1993, Chin-Hao moved to a small apartment with two friends. He also began to study English at night school. In 1994, Chin-Hao got a much better job in a small store that repaired and sold vacuum cleaners. The job was about an hour from his apartment, so he moved again, this time closer to work. In 1996, Chin-Hao began to study business at college part time. At school, he met a young woman, and soon they fell in love. In 1997, Chin-Hao got married, and he moved one more time. Now Chin-Hao and his wife are working, going to college, and saving for their first house.

Unit 15, page 147

B. Listen: getting ready Andre and Marie are planning to go camping this weekend. Listen to their conversation. Check the items that they already have. Circle the items that they need to buy or find.

Andre: I think we have all the big items—the tent, sleeping bags, stove, cooler, backpacks, fishing rod. And I have the matches. It's the little things like matches we always forget to bring.

Marie: I know. Let's go over everything. How about the camera?

Andre: Here it is, but I need to get film. And the compass?

Marie: I have it.

Andre: How about insect repellent?

Marie: Remember last year? We forgot to bring it and the mosquitoes ate us! I have to buy repellent and sun block, too.

Andre: Good. Where's the first-aid kit?

Marie: We need to find it. I think it's in the closet in the bathroom.

Andre: And what about the flashlight? Last year we forgot it.

Marie: I'm going to look for it now. What are we going to forget this year?

Unit 16, page 154

A. Listen: a working mother *Look at the picture and listen to this story about a working mother and her family.*

Pat and her husband, Bob, live in a two-bedroom home with their two children, Timmy and David. Timmy is three years old, and David is five. The mornings are always busy. At 5:45 the alarm clock rings, and Bob jumps out of bed. He uses the bathroom first and takes a shower. When he goes back into the bedroom, he wakes Pat up. After Pat gets up, she wakes up the children, then starts to make breakfast. Bob puts on a video for the boys because they're sleepy, and the video gives them a chance to wake up slowly. Bob gets dressed and eats breakfast. Before he leaves for work, he kisses the children and Pat good-bye. After Bob leaves, Pat eats breakfast with David and Timmy. After breakfast, she gets dressed and gets the boys ready for the day. Then she takes them out to the car, and the boys climb into their car seats. Before Pat starts the car, she buckles the boys in their car seats. Pat drives to the day care center, which is about fifteen minutes from home. As soon as she drops the kids off at the center, Pat drives to work. She's a hairstylist. She's often a little late for work, but her customers understand because they are mothers, too.

Unit 17, page 162

A. Listen: the robbery *Last night, Spike and Tina tried to rob a jewelry store. Repeat these verbs after your teacher and ask about any new words. Then look at the pictures and listen to the story.*

This is Spike. Spike's a burglar, and tonight he tried to rob a jewelry store. Spike's girlfriend, Tina, drove him to the jewelry store. She stayed in the car and watched for the police. Before Spike got out of the car, he put on black gloves, a mask, and a black hat. Spike walked around to the side of the store and broke the window with a baseball bat. After Spike broke the window, he climbed into the store. As soon as Spike stepped on the floor, an alarm rang. He quickly grabbed some diamonds and a pearl necklace, and put them in his bag. After he picked up the bag of jewelry, he jumped out of the window. When he got out of the store, he heard a police siren. As soon as he saw the police car, he began to run. When the police saw him, they chased him down an alley. Before Spike could climb over the wall, one of the policemen grabbed his leg. When Tina tried to drive away, another police car blocked her car. After the police caught Spike and Tina, they handcuffed them. The police put Spike and Tina into the police car and drove them to the police station.

Unit 18, page 170

A. Listen: the power went out *Look at the picture and listen to the story about the effects of the power blackout in the city. Draw a line from the name of each person or persons to their location when the power went out.*

It was 9:00 in the evening, and it had been a very hot day in the city. Everyone was trying to keep cool. Air conditioners and fans were working at full blast. Suddenly, the power went out. It was totally dark.

Bob and Mary Wilson and their children were watching a movie at the theater. When the power went out, the movie stopped. Ten minutes later, everyone had to go home. The manager gave everyone free tickets.

Becky was playing in the championship softball game when the lights on the field went out. The players waited in the dark for twenty minutes, but nothing happened. The teams and the fans were very disappointed, but everyone had to go home. They postponed the game.

Susan and her husband, Frank, were at a restaurant. They were celebrating Susan's promotion at work. When the lights went out, the waiters lit candles on all of the tables, and everyone continued eating in the romantic atmosphere.

Mike Tanaka was working at his office with his staff. When the power went out, no one could use the computers. His staff was very happy because they could all go home.

Officer Rodriguez was taking a coffee break when the power went out. All of the street lights went out. He and another officer got into their patrol car and drove around the neighborhood.